YOUR recipe could appear in our next cookbook!

Share your tried & true family favorites with us instantly at

www.gooseberrypatch.com

If you'd rather jot 'em down by hand, just mail this form to...

Gooseberry Patch • Cookbooks – Call for Recipes
2500 Farmers Dr., #110 • Columbus, OH 43235

If your recipe is selected for a book, you'll receive a FREE copy!

Please share only your original recipes or those that you have made your own over the years.

Recipe Name:

Number of Servings:

Any fond memories about this recipe? Special touches you like to add
or handy shortcuts?

Ingredients (include specific measurements):

Instructions (continue on back if needed):

Special Code: **cookbookspage**

Over ➤

Extra space for recipe if needed:

Tell us about yourself...

Your complete contact information is needed so that we can send you your FREE cookbook, if your recipe is published. Phone numbers and email addresses are kept private and will only be used if we have questions about your recipe.

Name:

Address:

City: State: Zip:

Email:

Daytime Phone:

Thank you! Vickie & Jo Ann

Gooseberry Patch

Quick & Easy Christmas

Gooseberry Patch
2500 Farmers Dr., #110
Columbus, OH 43235

www.gooseberrypatch.com

1·800·854·6673

Copyright 2011, Gooseberry Patch 978-1-936283-78-1
First Printing, March, 2011

Do you have a tried & true recipe...

tip, craft or memory that you'd like to see featured in a **Gooseberry
Patch** cookbook? Visit our website at **www.gooseberrypatch.com**
to share them with us instantly. If you'd rather jot them down by hand,
use the handy form in the front of this book and send them to...

Gooseberry Patch
Attn: Cookbook Dept.
2500 Farmers Dr., #110
Columbus, OH 43235

Don't forget to include the number of servings your recipe makes,
plus your name, address, phone number and email address.
If we select your recipe, your name will appear right along
with it...and you'll receive a **FREE** copy of the cookbook!

Table of Contents

Dedication

*For those who take
pleasure in preparing a
homestyle Christmas...and
make time to
enjoy it too!*

Appreciation

*A jolly thank-you to
everyone who shared
their family's favorite
holiday dishes!*

Breakfast & Brunch

Creamy Cinnamon Rolls

Sheila Plock
Boalsburg, PA

This makes a great breakfast treat anytime, but I always make it for Christmas morning. After placing rolls in the pan, you can cover with greased plastic wrap, refrigerate overnight, and let them rise until double, approximately two hours, the following morning.

1 loaf frozen white bread
   dough, thawed
2 T. butter, melted
2/3 c. brown sugar, packed
1/2 c. chopped nuts

1 t. cinnamon
1/2 c. whipping cream
2/3 c. powdered sugar
1 T. milk

On a lightly floured surface, roll dough into an 18-inch by 6-inch rectangle. Brush with melted butter. Combine brown sugar, nuts and cinnamon. Sprinkle evenly over dough. Roll up jelly-roll style, starting with the long side. Cut into 20 slices; arrange cut-side down in a greased 13"x9" baking pan. Cover and let rise until almost double, about 1-1/2 hours. Uncover and pour cream over rolls. Bake at 350 degrees for 25 to 30 minutes. Mix together powdered sugar and milk; drizzle over warm rolls. Makes 20.

A mulled cider sachet makes a warm and delicious beverage. Place these fragrant spices in a bouquet garni bag…2 cinnamon sticks, one piece star anise, 1/2 teaspoon whole cloves and 1/2 teaspoon whole allspice berries. Simmer the sachet in 2 quarts apple cider for 15 minutes. Remove the sachet and serve.

Cinnamon Biscuits

Linda Roper
Pine Mountain, GA

My children loved when I made these tasty treats
for breakfast on Sunday or Christmas.

2 T. plus 2 t. cinnamon
2 c. sugar
1/2 c. butter, melted

2 8-oz. tubes refrigerated
  biscuits

Mix together cinnamon and sugar in a medium bowl. Place melted butter in a separate bowl. Separate biscuits. Dip biscuits into butter, then into cinnamon mixture. Place biscuits on ungreased baking sheets. Bake at 375 degrees for 12 to 15 minutes, until golden. Makes 20.

I will always remember the Christmas we outsmarted Mom. Growing up, my brother Tom and I would wake at three o'clock on Christmas morning to sneak downstairs. We could never get our sister Charlotte up! One Christmas Mom swore we wouldn't make it downstairs in the middle of the night, so she set a booby trap for us. She tied pots and pans at the bottom of the stairs with string. We somehow got past without making a noise! My mother was so mad, but at the same time could not believe what we did. Sleepyhead Charlotte missed it all!

-Mel Chencharick, Julian, PA

Auntie Ruth's Shoo Fly Pie

Susan Boeggeman
Downingtown, PA

When I was a little girl, my mother wanted my sister and me to eat breakfast before seeing what Santa brought us. In order to accomplish this, my Auntie Ruth made Shoo Fly Pie. It worked! I am now fifty-one with three grown children and we still enjoy it for Christmas breakfast.

2-1/2 c. all-purpose flour
1 c. sugar
1/2 c. shortening
2 9-inch pie crusts
1 c. dark molasses

1-1/2 c. plus 2 t. hot water,
   divided
1 t. baking soda
2 eggs, beaten
cinnamon to taste

Mix together flour, sugar and shortening; set aside half of mixture. Spread remaining half evenly into bottom of pie crusts. In a separate bowl, combine molasses and 1-1/2 cups hot water. Dissolve baking soda in remaining water; add to molasses mixture. Blend in eggs. Pour evenly into pie crusts. Top with remaining flour mixture and sprinkle with cinnamon to taste. Bake at 450 degrees for 10 minutes; reduce heat to 350 degrees and bake an additional 15 minutes. Makes 2 pies, 6 servings each.

When measuring thick ingredients like molasses or honey, first spray the measuring cup with non-stick vegetable spray. The contents will slip right out and you'll get a more accurate measurement.

Hot Milk Cake

Tina George
El Dorado, AR

This cake tastes so good for a quick breakfast with a glass of cold milk. My family requests it for birthdays, instead of the regular frosted cake!

4 eggs
2 c. sugar
2-1/4 c. all-purpose flour
2-1/4 t. baking powder

1 t. vanilla extract
1-1/4 c. milk
2/3 c. butter

In a bowl, beat eggs with an electric mixer on high speed until thick, about 5 minutes. Gradually add sugar, beating until mixture is light and fluffy. In a separate bowl, combine flour and baking powder. Add flour mixture and vanilla to egg mixture; beat until smooth. Heat milk and butter in a saucepan over medium-low heat, until butter melts, stirring occasionally. Add milk mixture to egg mixture; blend well. Pour into a greased 13"x9" baking pan. Bake at 350 degrees for 30 to 35 minutes, until cake tests done. Cool on a wire rack before cutting. Makes 12 to 16 servings.

Personalize mugs to serve up toasty beverages at your holiday brunch. You'll find a rainbow of ceramic paints and markers at the craft shop. They're sweet keepsakes guests can take home as a reminder of the day!

Artichoke Squares

Deborah Patterson
Carmichael, CA

Right before we all open our gifts, I pop this dish in the oven.
The smell is wonderful! We can't wait to share brunch with my
extended family..such a happy time for all of us to be together again.

8 eggs
1 c. shredded sharp Cheddar
  cheese
1 onion, finely chopped
1 clove garlic, finely chopped

salt and pepper to taste
12 saltine crackers, crushed
2 6-oz. jars artichoke hearts,
  drained
Garnish: chopped fresh parsley

Beat eggs slightly in a large bowl. Add remaining ingredients except garnish; mix well. Pour into a lightly greased 11"x7" baking pan. Bake at 325 degrees for 25 minutes. Let cool slightly and sprinkle with parsley before serving. Makes 6 to 8 servings.

A hearty country breakfast for a chilly December morning!
Cook up frozen diced potatoes and onions in a cast-iron skillet,
then use the back of a spoon to make six wells. Break an egg
into each and bake at 350 degrees for 12 to 14 minutes,
until eggs are set. Add salt & pepper to taste and serve
piping hot, right from the skillet.

Lisa Ann's Crustless Quiche

Lisa Ann Panzino-DiNunzio
Vineland, NJ

This is such an easy, tasty and healthy quiche. It goes so quickly that I had to start making two!

1 T. safflower or canola oil
1 onion, thinly sliced
10-oz. pkg. frozen chopped
    spinach, thawed and drained
5 eggs, beaten

4 slices turkey bacon, crisply
    cooked and crumbled
3 c. shredded Cheddar cheese
1/4 t. sea salt
pepper to taste

Heat oil in a large skillet over medium-high heat. Cook onion, stirring occasionally, until tender and golden. Add spinach to skillet and continue cooking until excess liquid has evaporated. Remove from heat and set aside. In a large bowl, combine eggs, bacon, cheese, salt and pepper. Stir in onion mixture. Pour into a 9" pie plate that has been sprayed with non-stick vegetable spray. Bake at 350 degrees for 30 to 40 minutes, until eggs have set. Let stand 5 minutes before serving. Serves 6.

Dress up the beverage station at your holiday buffet.
Fasten a festive ribbon around a punch bowl and set it
in a fresh pine wreath...so pretty!

Weekend Pancakes

Sophia Graves
Okeechobee, FL

*At least one day during the weekend we have pancakes
in my house. When my niece and nephews visit they
always request these for breakfast.*

1-1/4 c. all-purpose flour
1 T. baking powder
1 T. sugar
1 T. butter, melted and cooled
   slightly

1 egg, beaten
1 t. vanilla extract
1 to 1-1/4 c. milk, divided

Mix together flour, baking powder and sugar in a large bowl. In a
separate bowl, stir together butter, egg, vanilla and one cup milk. Pour
butter mixture over flour mixture; mix well. If batter is too thick, add
additional milk to desired consistency. Pour batter by 1/4 cupfuls onto
a hot, lightly greased griddle. Cook until batter starts to bubble, about
3 minutes. Flip pancakes and cook an additional 2 to 3 minutes.
Serves 8.

Banana Pancake Topper

Macie Dilling
Raleigh, NC

*Perfect for a brunch! Top your favorite pancakes with a spoonful
of these luscious bananas and warmed syrup.*

2 bananas, peeled and sliced

2 T. butter, melted

In a large skillet over medium heat, cook bananas in butter for
2 to 3 minutes per side, until golden. Serves 4 to 6.

Oatmeal-Blueberry Pancakes

Joy Gamber
Mount Vernon, IL

Mmm...a pancake version of a favorite muffin!

1 c. biscuit baking mix
1 c. quick-cooking oats, uncooked
2 T. brown sugar, packed
3/4 c. milk

2 eggs, beaten
2 T. butter, melted and cooled slightly
1/2 c. blueberries

In a medium bowl, combine all ingredients except blueberries; mix well. Fold in blueberries. Pour batter by 1/4 cupfuls onto a hot, lightly greased griddle. Spread batter to 1/4-inch thickness. Cook on both sides until golden, turning when surface is bubbly and edges are slightly dry. Serves 8 to 10.

When you're making pancakes for a crowd,
keep them warm in a low-temperature oven.
Just arrange pancakes on a baking sheet,
set in the oven, then serve as needed.

Pepper Jack Frittata

Gladys Kielar
Perrysburg, OH

The red and green peppers look so festive at a holiday brunch.
Serve with salsa and sour cream for a "Feliz Navidad!"

1 red pepper, chopped
1 green pepper, chopped
1 t. fresh parsley, chopped

3/4 c. shredded Pepper Jack
  cheese
1-3/4 c. egg substitute

Sprinkle peppers, parsley and cheese into a 9" pie plate coated with butter-flavored non-stick vegetable spray. Pour egg substitute over all. Bake at 375 degrees for 30 minutes. Makes 4 servings.

Wrapping paper isn't just for presents. Tack up your favorite prints on kitchen cabinet doors or in the back of the china cabinet. Cut the paper to size and adhere with dots of reusable sticky putty. When it's time to come down, the paper will come off easily without damaging the surface.

14

4-Ingredient Breakfast Pizza

Kristin Pittis
Dennison, OH

My mother-in-law makes this every Christmas morning. For a change,
substitute real bacon bits for the sausage...or even use both!

2 8-oz. tubes refrigerated
   crescent rolls
2 eggs, beaten

7-oz. pkg. heat & serve pork
   breakfast sausage, sliced
1 c. shredded Cheddar cheese

Arrange crescent rolls in a rectangle on a lightly greased baking
sheet, pinching seams to seal. Spread eggs over crescent rolls.
Sprinkle sausage and cheese over top. Bake at 375 degrees for 15 to
20 minutes, until eggs are set and crust is golden. Makes 12 servings.

Welcome overnight guests by leaving special treats in their
rooms...wrap up scented soaps in plush washcloths, leave a few
mints on their pillows or set up a small coffee maker with
mugs and individual coffee packets for them to enjoy.

Yuletide Orange Smoothie

LaShelle Brown
Mulvane, KS

After we open our stockings, it's a family tradition to have this refreshing beverage along with our big breakfast.

12-oz. can frozen orange juice
    concentrate
2 c. milk
2 c. cold water

1 c. sugar
2 t. vanilla extract
16 to 18 ice cubes

Combine all ingredients in a blender. Blend about 30 seconds, or until smooth. Makes 8 servings.

Dress up glasses of Yuletide Orange Smoothie with a little sparkle. Tie tiny Christmas ornaments onto stemmed glasses with ribbon bows...so fun!

Fruited Orange Yogurt

Beth Bennett
Stratham, NH

*A smooth and crunchy, sweet and zingy breakfast
you can enjoy on-the-go.*

8-oz. container mascarpone
   cheese
32-oz. container plain yogurt
1/3 c. sugar

juice and zest of 2 oranges
Garnish: granola
blueberries, raspberries, sliced
   bananas

In a bowl, combine mascarpone cheese, yogurt and sugar. Stir in
juice and zest. Sprinkle granola over top. Serve with fresh fruit. Serves
4 to 6.

One of my favorite Christmas memories ever is from my
childhood. When he was about six, my little brother Jonathan
was bound and determined to see Santa Claus. The house we
grew up in didn't have a fireplace so Jonathan was convinced
Santa had to come through the front door. After we all went to
sleep, he grabbed the warm and cozy afghan our YiaYia
(Greek for grandmother) had knitted for him. He curled up in
a chair in the living room watching the door. When I woke up
Christmas morning, I found him asleep in the chair. I ran and
got my parents and we just all watched him sleep for a few
minutes...so small and cute! Even though I was only eight years
old, I will always remember how that Christmas magic was in the
heart of a sweet little boy who only wanted a glimpse of Santa!

-Kristen DeSimone, Peabody, MA

Brandi's Egg & Spinach Bake

Brandi Talton
Guyton, GA

I created this recipe for my husband.
So flavorful and filling!

10 eggs, beaten
1/4 c. whipping cream
1/4 c. milk
2 t. pepper, or to taste

1/8 t. garlic salt
2 c. spinach
2 tomatoes, diced
1 c. deli ham, diced

Mix together all ingredients in a large bowl. Pour into a 12"x9" baking pan that has been sprayed with non-stick vegetable spray. Bake, uncovered, at 350 degrees for 30 minutes, or until eggs are set. Serves 6.

At Christmas, all roads lead home.

–Marjorie Holmes

Girlfriends' Cheesy Egg Bake

Linda Murray
Brentwood, NH

*My friend shared this with me several years ago. My daughter
has now taken over the honors of having the family to
Christmas breakfast at her house and serving this dish.*

2 10-3/4 oz. cans cream of
   chicken soup
1/2 c. milk
4 t. onion, grated
1 t. mustard
1-1/4 c. shredded extra-sharp
   Cheddar cheese

1 doz. eggs
1/4 to 1/2 c. butter, softened
1 loaf French bread, sliced
   1/2-inch thick
Optional: chopped fresh parsley

In a saucepan over medium heat, combine soup, milk, onion and
mustard; stir constantly until heated through. Remove from heat; stir
in cheese until melted. Pour half of soup mixture into a lightly greased
13"x9" baking pan. Break eggs onto the top of the soup mixture.
Spoon remaining soup mixture around eggs. Butter both sides of
bread slices; stand bread around edges of pan. Bake, uncovered, at
350 degrees for 30 minutes, or until eggs are set. Sprinkle with
parsley, if desired. Makes 12 servings.

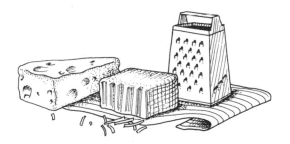

Cheese toast is delicious alongside savory breakfast dishes...and a
snap to make on a countertop grill. Spread softened butter over
slices of French or sourdough bread, grill until golden,
then sprinkle with your favorite cheese.

So-Easy Caramel Rolls

Amy Teets
Saint Peters, MO

A simple breakfast I like serving to company! If you wish, sprinkle chopped nuts on top of the ice cream topping before adding the rolls.

1/4 c. butter
12-1/4 oz. jar caramel ice cream
   topping

2 8-oz. tubes refrigerated
   crescent rolls

Place butter in a 13"x9" baking pan and place in a 375-degree oven until melted. Once melted, add ice cream topping and mix well. Without unrolling the dough, remove dough from tubes. Cut each section into 6 rolls and place cut-side down in pan. Bake at 375 degrees for 20 to 25 minutes. Immediately invert onto a serving plate. Makes one dozen.

Little extras for Christmas morning...a small wrapped
gift at each place setting, soft holiday music in the
background and no lights allowed except those
on the tree. So magical!

Auntie Kay Kay's Sticky Buns

Jen Sell
Farmington, MN

Everyone loves when my Auntie Kay Kay visits! She always makes these sticky buns that are ready to bake in the morning. She didn't hesitate when I asked her for the recipe...now I can make them when she's not here.

2 loaves frozen sweet bread
   dough
1/2 c. cinnamon-sugar
1/2 c. butter, softened

1/2 c. sugar
1/2 c. brown sugar, packed
1/2 c. vanilla ice cream

Place bread dough into a lightly greased 13"x9" baking pan. Cover pan with plastic wrap that has been sprayed with non-stick vegetable spray; thaw in the refrigerator overnight. In the morning, cut dough into bite-size pieces; coat in cinnamon-sugar. Return buns to pan. Melt butter, sugars and ice cream in a saucepan over medium-low heat; stir until smooth. Pour over buns. Bake at 400 degrees for 20 minutes. Serves 6 to 8.

Offer guests fun toppers for their coffees...flavored creamers, mini chocolate chips and fluffy whipped topping. And don't forget peppermint sticks for stirrers. Yum!

Linen & Lace

Marie Hulse
Gardnerville, NV

This French toast dish is a traditional Christmas breakfast in my husband's family. My sister-in-law and I prepare this recipe every Christmas Eve. We have so much fun laughing and catching up on the past year! With breakfast out of the way, we can enjoy Christmas morning together.

1 loaf French bread, sliced
   1-inch thick
8 eggs, beaten
3/4 t. salt
3 c. milk

4 t. sugar
1 T. vanilla extract
2 T. butter, melted
Garnish: maple syrup

Arrange bread slices in a single layer in a well-greased 13"x9" baking pan. Mix remaining ingredients except butter and garnish; pour over bread. Cover with aluminum foil and refrigerate overnight. In the morning, drizzle with melted butter and bake, uncovered, at 350 degrees for 40 minutes. Let stand 2 to 3 minutes; serve with maple syrup. Makes 8 to 12 servings.

Buttermilk Syrup

Karen Ensign
Providence, UT

A yummy syrup served over pancakes or waffles. You can substitute 1/2 cup milk combined with one tablespoon vinegar for the buttermilk.

2 T. butter, softened
3/4 c. sugar
1 t. light corn syrup

1/2 c. buttermilk
1/2 t. baking soda
1 t. vanilla extract

In a saucepan over medium-high heat, boil all ingredients except vanilla for one minute. Remove from heat and stir in vanilla. Cover and store in refrigerator. Makes about one cup.

Strawberry Cheesecake French Toast

Sharon Larson
Collinsville, IL

I serve this treat when my grandkids come to spend the night. And in the summer, it's a way of saying "thank you" for helping Gramma pick strawberries.

8-oz. container ricotta cheese
3 T. powdered sugar
1 t. vanilla extract
1 loaf French bread, sliced
   1/2-inch thick
2 eggs, beaten

1 c. milk
2 c. strawberries, hulled and
   sliced
Garnish: maple syrup, additional
   powdered sugar

In a small bowl, combine ricotta, powdered sugar and vanilla. Spread 2 tablespoons on each of 8 slices of bread; top each slice with remaining bread to form a sandwich. In a bowl, beat together eggs and milk; soak sandwiches for one to 2 minutes per side. Cook on a hot, greased griddle for 5 minutes on each side, or until golden and heated through. Serve with strawberries. Garnish with syrup and additional powdered sugar. Makes 8 servings.

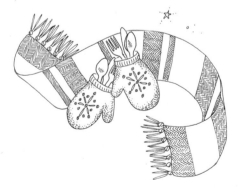

If your basket of winter accessories is overflowing with scarves, put them to work as a tree skirt. Arrange in a pinwheel fashion around the tree and secure with safety pins.

Creamed Eggs on Biscuits

Jonna Jackson
Quincy, IL

The first time I heard of this dish was the first Christmas I spent with my husband's family. It's now our family's tradition and often requested for Sunday breakfast throughout the year.

12 eggs, hard-boiled and peeled
1/2 c. butter
3 to 4 T. all-purpose flour
5-oz. can evaporated milk

1 c. water
3/4 to 1-1/2 c. milk
warm biscuits or toast

Slice eggs both ways with an egg slicer; set aside. Melt butter in a saucepan over medium-low heat. Stir in flour. Add evaporated milk, stirring constantly. Add water while continuing to stir. As sauce begins to thicken, add enough milk to desired consistency. Stir in eggs; heat through. Serve over split biscuits or toast. Serves 6.

Doughnut hole kabobs...what a delicious idea! Slide bite-size doughnut holes onto wooden skewers and stand the skewers in a tall vase or cookie tin for easy serving.

Make-Ahead Morning Casserole

Susie Backus
Gooseberry Patch

This recipe is so easy to make ahead and perfect for when company comes. It's enjoyed by my family for most holidays!

8 eggs, beaten
3 c. milk
1 lb. ground pork sausage,
    browned and drained
10 slices bread, torn into
    bite-size pieces
2 c. shredded Cheddar cheese

2 c. sliced fresh mushrooms or
    4-oz. can mushroom pieces
    and stems, drained
2 T. butter, melted
2 T. all-purpose flour
1 T. dry mustard
salt and pepper to taste

In a large bowl, combine all ingredients; mix well. Spoon into a greased 13"x9" baking pan. Cover with aluminum foil and refrigerate overnight. Bake, covered, at 350 degrees for 60 to 75 minutes, until a knife inserted in center comes out clean. Makes 8 to 10 servings.

Tuck napkin-wrapped cutlery into a child-size mitten to lay at each place setting...how sweet!

25

Pineapple Upside-Down Biscuits

Billye Barrow
Cleveland, TX

My good friend Myrtie shared this recipe with me.
So simple and delicious...we love it!

10-oz. can crushed pineapple,
   drained and juice reserved
1/2 c. light brown sugar, packed
1/4 c. butter, melted

1/4 c. chopped pecans
10 maraschino cherries
10-oz. tube refrigerated
   buttermilk biscuits

Combine pineapple, sugar, butter and pecans; mix well. Spray
10 muffin cups with non-stick vegetable spray; place a cherry in the
bottom of each muffin cup. Divide pineapple mixture evenly among
the cups. Place one biscuit in each cup on top of pineapple mixture.
Spoon one teaspoon of reserved pineapple juice over each biscuit.
Bake at 350 degrees for 12 to 15 minutes, until golden. Cool for
2 minutes. Invert pan over plate to release biscuits. Serve warm.
Makes 10.

Bring country charm right into
the kitchen with a mini
Christmas tree! Trim it with
gingerbread cookies, tea strainers,
cookie cutters, toy-size kitchen
utensils and garlands of
cinnamon sticks and
dried apple slices.

Breakfast & Brunch

Gooey Honey Biscuits

Cheri Emery
Quincy, IL

Indulge in a little quiet time with a steaming mug of coffee and warm-from-the oven goodies.

2 c. all-purpose flour
4 t. baking powder
1/2 t. salt
2 t. sugar
1 t. cream of tartar

1/2 c. shortening
2/3 c. milk
1/4 c. butter, melted
1/3 c. honey

Blend together flour, baking powder, salt, sugar and cream of tartar in a large bowl. Cut in shortening with pastry blender or 2 knives, until mixture resembles cornmeal. Mix in milk. Turn out dough onto a lightly floured surface and knead 12 to 15 times. Break dough into 1/3 cup-size pieces. Roll pieces into balls; pat to 1/2-inch thickness. Place biscuits on ungreased baking sheets and brush with melted butter. Bake at 450 degrees for 10 to 12 minutes. While biscuits are baking, place honey and remaining butter in a saucepan over medium heat; bring to a boil. Remove honey mixture from heat and brush over biscuits before serving. Makes about one dozen.

Offer a quick & creamy salmon spread for brunch. Combine an 8-ounce package of cream cheese, 2 tablespoons prepared horseradish, 2 tablespoons chopped fresh dill and salt & pepper to taste. Fold in 1/4 pound of chopped smoked salmon and serve with vegetables and crackers.

Blueberry Muffin Cake

Amy Cassidy
Morganton, NC

A nice change from blueberry muffins.
Wonderful for breakfast or anytime.

2 7-oz. pkgs. blueberry
   muffin mix
1 c. plus 3 T. milk, divided

1/2 c. powdered sugar
1 t. lemon extract

In a bowl, use a spoon to stir together dry muffin mix and one cup milk until well blended. Pour batter into a greased 8"x8" baking pan. Bake at 400 degrees for 18 to 20 minutes. Use a fork to poke holes into warm cake. Mix together remaining milk, powdered sugar and extract. Pour glaze over warm cake. Let stand 15 minutes before serving. Makes 9 servings.

Enjoy the taste of homemade muffins even on a busy morning!
Freeze baked muffins in a freezer-safe bag, then remove
as needed and let thaw in the refrigerator overnight.

Breakfast & Brunch

Busy Morning Banana Bread

Laura Justice
Indianapolis, IN

Super easy and freezes well. Just pull from the freezer the night before and it will be ready for your busy morning!

3 ripe bananas, mashed
3 eggs, beaten
1/2 c. butter, melted

1 T. vanilla extract
1/2 c. water
18-1/2 oz. pkg. yellow cake mix

In a large bowl, blend together bananas, eggs, butter, vanilla and water. Gradually add in dry cake mix. Beat for 4 minutes. Pour batter into 2 greased 9"x5" loaf pans. Bake at 350 degrees for 40 minutes. Increase temperature to 400 degrees and bake an additional 5 to 10 minutes, until tops are golden. Makes 2 loaves.

Sweet breads aren't just for breakfast! For yummy lunchbox sandwiches, top slices of pumpkin or banana bread with peanut butter, jam, flavored cream cheese or apple slices.

Breakfast Berry Parfait

Michelle Case
Yardley, PA

So pretty served in a parfait or champagne glass!

1 c. strawberries, hulled
1/2 c. raspberries
1/4 c. blackberries

1 c. bran & raisin cereal
6-oz. container strawberry
   yogurt

Combine berries in a bowl. Top with cereal. Spoon yogurt over all. Serves 2.

When I was little, family "videos" were shot on 8mm film. I can still see the bright "movie" lights in the living room downstairs that signaled Santa had arrived. My younger brothers and I would wait eagerly at the top of the stairs, peeking through the banisters and squealing with excitement until we were finally called to come down. How we ran down the stairs to see what presents awaited us as Dad filmed the joy of Christmas morning! Those home movies still make us (and our children!) laugh and bring back warm memories of an old-fashioned family tradition.

-Mary Simpson, Brick, NJ

Winter Fruit Salad

Nancy Girard
Chesapeake, VA

Perfect to make during the winter months when fresh fruit is not as abundant. It can be made a day ahead for a holiday brunch.

1/2 c. sugar
2 T. cornstarch
20 oz. can pineapple chunks,
    drained and 3/4 c. juice
    reserved
1/3 c. orange juice

1 T. lemon juice
11-oz. can mandarin oranges,
    drained
3 to 4 red and green apples,
    cored and chopped
2 to 3 bananas, sliced

In a saucepan, combine sugar and cornstarch. Add reserved pineapple juice, orange juice and lemon juice. Cook and stir over medium heat until thick and bubbly; cook and stir one minute longer. Remove from heat; set aside. In a bowl, combine pineapple, oranges, apples and bananas. Pour warm sauce over fruit; stir gently to coat. Cover and refrigerate to cool before serving. Makes 12 servings.

Craft a fun snowball wreath that won't melt!
Hot-glue fuzzy white pompoms over a foam wreath,
then top it with a simple bow.

Christmas Morning Casserole

Kristin Smith
Bartlesville, OK

I remember visiting my grandma on Christmas morning and opening presents with her. She always fixed this casserole for us to eat. Now I make it for my family!

1 lb. ground pork sausage,
   browned and drained
6 eggs, beaten
1 c. shredded Colby Jack cheese

2 c. milk
1 t. dry mustard
1 c. biscuit baking mix
1 t. dried oregano

Mix together all ingredients and pour into a greased 13"x9" baking pan. Cover and refrigerate overnight. Bake, uncovered, at 350 degrees for one hour. Serves 6.

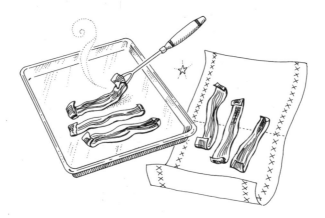

Make fancy bacon curls to garnish breakfast plates.
Fry bacon until browned but not crisp, immediately
roll up slices and fasten each with a toothpick.
Drain on paper towels. Mmm!

Savory Christmas Breakfast

Lori Ragalis
New Britain, CT

This make-ahead recipe bakes while you empty the stockings and open presents.

7 slices white bread, crusts
   removed
1 c. shredded Cheddar cheese
6 eggs, beaten
3 c. milk

1/2 t. salt
1/4 t. pepper
1 t. dry mustard
3 slices bacon

Tear bread slices. Mix together bread crumbs and cheese; transfer to a greased 12"x9" baking pan. Combine eggs and milk; pour over top. Stir together salt, pepper and mustard; sprinkle over egg mixture. Place bacon on top. Cover and refrigerate overnight. Bake, uncovered, at 350 degrees for 50 to 55 minutes, until bacon is crisp and casserole is set. Serves 6.

Put a slow cooker to work at the breakfast buffet...set on low, it can keep sausage gravy, scrambled eggs or other breakfast foods piping-hot and delicious.

Treasure Puffs

Bonnie Bichl
Platteville, WI

I made these on Christmas morning for my family many years ago. No one could go into the living room until Treasure Puffs were done! If you prefer, use eight bite-size candy bars instead of the large candy bar.

8-oz. tube refrigerated crescent   1/4 c. butter, melted
   rolls
2.11-oz. chocolate-covered
   nougat candy bar,
   unwrapped

Divide crescent rolls into 8 sections. Cut candy bar into 8 pieces. Wrap each piece of candy with a crescent roll. Dip rolls into melted butter; turn to coat. Place on an ungreased baking sheet. Bake at 350 degrees for about 10 minutes, or until golden. Makes 8.

As Christmas nears, plan a family slumber party! Set up quilts and sleeping bags around the tree, pass around lots of snacks and watch a holiday movie. Before falling asleep, read "The Night Before Christmas" with only the tree lights on.

Pancake Cookies

Pat Hancock
Hawthorne, NJ

My mother made these cookies every year by the dozens...everyone went nuts about them! Great for breakfast parties, kids' breakfasts or to give as holiday cookies. You can substitute chocolate hazelnut spread for the jam or preserves.

3 eggs, beaten
1-1/2 c. milk
1/2 c. water
1 T. butter, melted
2 T. sugar
1 T. baking powder

1/8 t. salt
2-3/4 c. all-purpose flour
10-oz. jar favorite-flavor jam or
    preserves
Garnish: 1 c. powdered sugar

In a large bowl, blend together eggs, milk, water and butter. In a separate bowl, combine sugar, baking powder, salt and flour. Gradually beat sugar mixture into egg mixture; blend well. Heat a griddle pan over medium heat and spray with non-stick vegetable spray. Spoon batter into 2-1/2 to 3-inch circles on griddle. Cook pancakes 2 to 3 minutes per side; set aside to cool. Spread a thin layer of jam or preserves on each cooled pancake. Roll up pancakes. Line up tightly on a plate to keep from unrolling. Sprinkle with powdered sugar. Makes one dozen.

Original, personalized ornaments are so easy to craft! Attach alphabet stickers to matte-finish Christmas ball ornaments, spelling family names or holiday expressions like "JOY" or "PEACE." For sparkle, hot-glue tiny jewels or sequins onto ornaments.

Texas Steak Bake

Nicole Manley
Great Lakes, IL

A hearty morning dish to get you going!

8-oz. tube refrigerated crescent
    rolls
6-oz. pkg. fully-cooked beef
    steak strips
4-oz. can mushroom stems and
    pieces, drained

1/2 onion, chopped
1/2 green pepper, chopped
1/2 c. shredded Cheddar cheese
5 eggs, beaten
1/2 c. milk
salt and pepper to taste

Arrange crescent rolls in the bottom of a 13"x9" baking pan that has
been sprayed with non-stick vegetable spray; press together seams.
Top crust with steak, mushrooms, onion and green pepper. Sprinkle
cheese on top. Beat together eggs, milk, salt and pepper; pour over
cheese. Bake, uncovered, at 425 degrees for 20 to 25 minutes.
Serves 6 to 8.

Stem and seed a green pepper in a flash...hold the pepper
upright on a cutting board. Use a sharp knife to slice each
of the sides from the pepper. You'll then have four
large seedless pieces ready for chopping!

Snacks & Appetizers

Doodads

Abigail Smith
Worthington, OH

My grandmother always had this snack stashed away for us when we'd visit. She has been gone for more than twenty years now, but I make this special mix for my dad each Christmas as a treat for him in memory of his mother.

4 c. pretzel sticks
2 c. bite-size honey-flavored
    corn cereal
6 c. combination of bite-size
    crispy wheat, rice and corn
    cereal squares
3 c. bite-size sweetened graham
    cereal squares

3 c. mixed nuts
1 c. butter, melted
1/4 c. plus 2 T. brown sugar,
    packed
1/4 c. Worcestershire sauce

In a very large bowl, mix pretzels, cereals and nuts. Spread into 2 ungreased 15"x10" jelly-roll pans. In a small bowl, mix together remaining ingredients, stirring until brown sugar is dissolved. Pour over pretzel mix; toss to coat. Bake at 250 degrees for one hour, stirring every 15 minutes. Spread on wax paper to cool, about 15 minutes. Store in an airtight container. Makes about 18 cups.

Here's a simple appetizer with the colors of the holidays. Roll thin slices of roasted red pepper around a basil leaf and a mini mozzarella ball. Secure with decorative toothpicks and serve on your favorite tray.

Christmas Crunch

Kathleen Felton
Fairfax, IA

Crunchy and sweet, this snack is a holiday favorite with our family!

1/2 c. butter
1 c. brown sugar, packed
1/2 c. chopped pecans
2-1/2 c. corn flake cereal

In a saucepan over medium-low heat, melt butter. Stir in sugar; bring to a boil, then immediately remove from heat. Add pecans and cereal; toss to coat. Spread on wax paper to cool. Break apart and store in an airtight container. Makes about 2 cups.

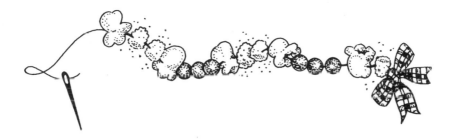

My fondest Christmas memory is of my dad and me going to our garage with three simple things...fishing line, cranberries and popped popcorn. We sat for hours stringing the popcorn and berries onto the fishing line. After hanging our "labor of love" on our beautiful evergreen tree, Dad and I watched all the birds have their Christmas feast. Even though Dad has since passed away, so many wonderful memories remain...including his love for the simple yet significant things.

-Melissa Knight, Athens, AL

Hanky Pankys

Eleanor Dionne
Beverly, MA

*An easy recipe we have loved for many years. These can be
made ahead and frozen before baking...just thaw and
pop in the oven when you're ready!*

1 lb. ground beef
1 lb. ground Italian pork
   sausage
1 t. dried oregano
1/2 t. garlic powder

salt and pepper to taste
1 t. Worcestershire sauce
16-oz. pkg. pasteurized process
   cheese spread, cubed
1 loaf sliced party rye bread

In a skillet over medium heat, brown ground beef and Italian sausage;
drain. Stir in seasonings and Worcestershire sauce. Add cheese
spread; mix and heat until completely melted. Spread onto party rye
slices. Place on lightly greased baking sheets. Bake at 350 degrees for
10 minutes, or until hot and bubbly. Serves 8 to 10.

Stock up on festive party napkins, candles and table decorations
at holiday sales. Then tuck them away in a big box...you'll be
all set to turn a casual get-together into a party.

Pepper Corn Cups

Kimberly Ascroft
Merritt Island, FL

*I first made this appetizer for a Christmas party. It has
turned into an anytime favorite!*

8-oz. round Brie cheese
16-oz. pkg. frozen corn, thawed
1 red pepper, diced

1 orange pepper, diced
3 2-oz. pkgs. frozen mini phyllo
   shells, thawed

Trim and discard rind from Brie; cut Brie into cubes. Mix together corn
and peppers. Place mini phyllo shells on lightly greased baking sheets;
evenly divide corn mixture into shells. Place one cube of Brie on each
shell. Bake at 350 degrees for 5 to 8 minutes. Makes 3-3/4 dozen.

Grandma always had a handmade potholder that was too
special to use. Turn it into a handy eyeglasses case...simply fold
together, with the tab at top, and stitch along two edges.

Swedish Meatballs

Jane Granger
Manteno, IL

I always make a double batch of these meatballs! And I triple the sauce recipe, so if any meatballs are left over, there will be enough sauce to reheat them in.

1-1/2 lbs. smoked ham, finely diced	2 c. dry bread crumbs
1 lb. ground pork sausage	2 eggs, beaten
	1 c. milk

Mix together all ingredients and roll into 1-1/2 to 2-inch balls. Place on an ungreased 13"x9" baking pan or a large roaster. Pour Sauce over meatballs and bake, uncovered, at 325 degrees for 1-1/2 hours, turning meatballs every 30 minutes. Makes about 2-1/2 dozen.

Sauce:

1/2 c. water	1-1/2 c. brown sugar, packed
1/2 c. vinegar	1 T. dry mustard

Mix together all ingredients in a small saucepan over medium-low heat until smooth.

Let your slow cooker be your party helper, keeping meatballs or chicken wings warm and cheesy dips hot and bubbly!

Snacks & Appetizers

Summer Sausage

LaShelle Brown
Mulvane, KS

*My mother always makes this savory treat at Christmas and includes
half of a log on everyone's goodie trays! Look for curing salt
in your grocer's canning and preserving section.*

2 lbs. lean ground beef
2 T. pepper
2 T. curing salt
1-1/2 t. smoke-flavored cooking
    sauce

1/8 t. garlic powder
1/4 t. onion powder

Mix together all ingredients. Shape into 3 logs about 1-1/2 inch in
diameter. Wrap each log very tightly in plastic wrap; refrigerate for
24 hours. Remove plastic wrap. Place on a lightly greased baking
sheet; bake, uncovered, at 300 degrees for 1-1/4 hours. Keep
refrigerated. Makes 3 logs.

The crisp green of limes is so nice at Christmas. Fill a clear
glass canister or large jar with an assortment of whole limes,
lime slices and sparkling water. A centerpiece in a snap!

Chutney-Topped Brie

Kathy Harris
Valley Center, KS

I was a little worried about trying Brie because I thought there was some mystery to it. To my surprise, I found an easy recipe and it turned out great! We enjoyed this over the holidays and will definitely add it to our list of family favorites.

8-oz. round Brie cheese
1/4 c. apricot or cranberry
   chutney

2 T. chopped almonds or
   walnuts
assorted crackers

Trim and discard rind from top of Brie round, leaving a 1/4-inch border. Place Brie in an ungreased ovenproof serving dish; top with chutney. Bake, uncovered, at 400 degrees for 10 minutes, or until it appears melted. Watch closely to ensure it doesn't seep out. Toast nuts in a small non-stick skillet over medium-low heat, stirring often, for 2 to 3 minutes. Sprinkle nuts over Brie. Serve warm with assorted crackers. Serves 8 to 10.

Toast a large batch of nuts and keep them on hand
for a tasty dessert garnish.

Secret Trail Cheese Ball

Becca Jones
Jackson, TN

A different twist to the cheese ball family! I discovered this in a small-town newspaper as part of someone's Christmas tradition. I have used it many times over the years...guests always ask for the recipe.

8-oz. can crushed pineapple, drained
2 8-oz. pkgs. cream cheese, softened

1/3 c. raisins
1/2 c. chopped dates
1/2 c. chopped pecans
round buttery crackers

Mix together all ingredients except pecans and crackers; blend well. Shape into a ball. Roll in chopped pecans. Refrigerate until serving time. Serve with crackers. Serves 10.

Instead of wrapping a cheese ball in plastic for gift-giving, spoon it into a pretty canning jar with a zinc lid, then tie on a spreader.

Feta Squares

Jane Kirsch
Weymouth, MA

*Pass around a tray of these snacks at your next get-together or
serve with a tossed salad for a special lunch.*

8-oz. container crumbled
  feta cheese
8-oz. pkg. cream cheese,
  softened
2 T. olive oil
3 cloves garlic, finely chopped

1 loaf sliced party pumpernickel
  bread
1 pt. grape tomatoes, halved
2 to 3 T. fresh chives, finely
  chopped

In a bowl, mix feta cheese, cream cheese, olive oil and garlic. Spread
mixture on pumpernickel slices. Place on ungreased baking sheets.
Top each square with a tomato half; sprinkle with chives. Bake at
350 degrees for 15 minutes. Serves 8 to 10.

Use tiered cake stands for bite-size appetizers...so handy,
and they take up less space on the buffet table than
setting out several serving platters.

Zippy Snack Crackers

Tammy Rogers
Gordonsville, VA

*My kids and all of their friends absolutely love
these crackers for munching.*

8-oz. pkg. oyster crackers
3/4 c. oil
1-oz. env. ranch salad dressing
   mix

1 t. garlic powder
1 t. lemon pepper
1 T. dill weed

Place crackers in an ungreased 13"x9" baking pan. Pour oil into a
2-cup measuring cup; add remaining ingredients and whisk to mix
well. Pour mixture over crackers; stir to coat evenly. Bake at
200 degrees for approximately 20 minutes, stirring every 5 minutes
with a plastic spatula. Cool; store in an airtight container. Makes
10 to 12 servings.

Decorate a frosty glass jar to fill with holiday goodies.
Choose a clear glass jar and press on star or snowflake-shaped
stickers as desired. Following package directions, apply etching
cream to jar, covering completely. Peel off stickers when
finished to reveal your one-of-a-kind design!

Jalapeño Puffers

Pia Cummins
Captain Cook, HI

I ran out of ingredients to make batter once and found a long-lost package of puff pastry in the freezer. I figured, why not try this instead? It's fast and less messy than regular batter...plus you don't need a fryer!

9 to 12 jalapeño peppers
8-oz. pkg. sharp Cheddar cheese
8-oz. pkg. cream cheese

17.3-oz. pkg. frozen puff pastry,
   thawed

Cut jalapeños in half lengthwise; remove stems, seeds and ribs. Cut cheeses into strips to fit inside jalapeños. In each jalapeño, layer a strip of Cheddar, then a layer of cream cheese. Cut the puff pastry dough into 9 to 12 squares; stretch to fit around jalapeños. Wrap a dough square around each jalapeño; overlap seams and pinch closed. Place on ungreased baking sheets. Bake at 400 degrees for 15 to 20 minutes, until golden. Let cool on wire racks for a few minutes before serving. Makes 9 to 12.

Decorations all through the house...even the bath!
Lace a holiday ribbon through each hole of your shower
curtain and tie a bow over the rod.

Holiday Ham Cracker Spread
Sheryl Araujo-Pedroza
Wixom, MI

*My aunt shared this recipe with me. I make it every year
at my daughter's request. She loves the flavor and I love
how it's very simple to make.*

2 8-oz. pkgs. cream cheese,
   softened
1 T. garlic, minced
1 onion, minced
6 to 8 thin slices deli ham,
   chopped

8-oz. pkg. finely shredded
   Cheddar cheese, divided
assorted crackers

Place cream cheese in a bowl; add garlic, onion, ham and half of
cheese. Mix well and shape into a ball. Place remaining cheese on a
plate; roll the ball in cheese to coat. Cover and refrigerate for 2 to
3 hours. Remove from refrigerator about an hour before serving to
soften slightly. Serve with crackers. Serves 8 to 10.

Dress up plain pillar candles in an instant...press in fancy
brass upholstery tacks or map pins to form spirals, stars,
stripes or other simple patterns.

Crab & Grapefruit Cocktail

Kathy Daynes
Littleton, CO

This is a recipe that my mother-in-law Tony would serve on Christmas Eve. It is an unusual recipe, one that most people haven't ever tried. It's so delicious, some might require a spoon! For the best flavor, refrigerate for the full twenty-four hours.

46-oz. can tomato juice
24-oz. bottle catsup
juice of 2 lemons
6-oz. can crabmeat, well drained

2 c. grapefruit sections, cut into
  bite-size pieces
salt and pepper to taste
shredded wheat crackers

Mix together all ingredients except crackers in a large bowl. Cover and chill 4 to 24 hours. Serve with shredded wheat crackers. Serves 12.

Make a recipe book of the best handed-down family favorites.
Tie it all up with a bow and slip a family photo in
the front...a gift to be treasured.

Averill's Holiday Punch

Carol Slavens
Jackson, OH

This is the easiest and best recipe! My mother Averill always made it for our Christmas Eve parties. With such a beautiful pink color, it can be served at weddings and occasions all year long!

1-qt. container raspberry
   sherbet, slightly thawed and
   divided

2-ltr. bottle lemon-lime soda,
   chilled and divided

Place half of sherbet in a punch bowl or large container. Add half of soda; stir. Repeat with remaining sherbet, then soda. Mix well. Serves 8.

Add a bit of sparkle and spice to holiday drinks...tie a little ornament or bauble onto a cinnamon stick. The cinnamon stick is a great stirrer, while the ornament dangles over your mug of hot cocoa, mulled cider or creamy eggnog.

Easy Peanut Wontons

Yvonne Coleman
Statesville, NC

*I came up with this recipe one day when I was in the mood for wontons.
I'm not a big fan of cabbage, so I went to the kitchen and played with
some ingredients I had on hand. I chose four of my favorites and added
soy sauce and sugar. Yum!*

1 c. carrots, peeled and
   shredded
1 c. zucchini, shredded
1 c. peanuts, finely ground
1 c. mushrooms, finely chopped
1/2 t. sugar

3 T. light soy sauce
16-oz. pkg. wonton wrappers
oil for deep frying
12-oz. bottle sweet-and-sour
   sauce or duck sauce

Mix together carrots, zucchini, peanuts, mushrooms, sugar and soy
sauce in a medium bowl. Mixture should be slightly moist and stick
together. Place one tablespoon mixture near the center of each wonton
wrapper. Fold wrappers according to package directions. Moisten ends
of wrappers and roll to seal. In a deep fryer, heat oil to 3-inch depth.
Drop wontons, one at a time, into hot oil; fry for approximately 2 to
3 minutes, turning until golden. Remove from oil; drain on paper
towels. Serve warm with desired sauce. Makes about 2 dozen.

Spruce up glass ornaments that have lost their shine!
Simply brush with craft glue and sprinkle with fine
glitter. Add hanging loops of colorful ribbon or
metallic cord...better than new!

Snacks & Appetizers

Chicky Popovers

Deanna Lyons
Roswell, GA

These elegant appetizers are surprisingly simple to make and oh-so yummy!

8-oz. pkg. cream cheese, softened
3 boneless, skinless chicken breasts, cooked and shredded
1-1/2 t. sesame seed
1/4 t. dried parsley
1 T. onion, minced

1 t. garlic, minced
1/2 c. spinach, finely chopped
Optional: 1/2 c. mushrooms, finely chopped
salt and pepper to taste
2 8-oz. tubes refrigerated crescent rolls

In a medium bowl, combine all ingredients except crescent rolls; mix well. Open crescent rolls but do not separate into triangles. Instead pair triangles to form 8 squares. Pinch seams together. Spoon chicken mixture evenly over the squares. Fold up corners into center, layering like flower petals so each roll is sealed. Place popovers on a lightly greased baking sheet. Bake at 350 degrees for 12 to 15 minutes, until golden and heated through. Makes 8 servings.

Host a snack & swap party... kids are welcome! Have everyone bring unwrapped toys and trinkets from home that have been lightly used. Parents can enjoy snacks and conversation while the children play and trade toys.

Mom's Dill Bread Bowl

Charlene Blackburn
Overland Park, KS

Decorate the top of this creamy dip with a sprig of fresh dill formed into the shape of a Christmas tree. Then cut out a carrot star for the top and use finely chopped red and yellow peppers for ornaments. How pretty!

1 round loaf pumpernickel bread	1 T. dried parsley
1 c. sour cream	2 T. dried, minced onion
1 c. mayonnaise	1 t. garlic powder
1 T. dill weed	assorted cut-up vegetables
1-1/2 t. seasoning salt	

Hollow out the center of bread loaf; set aside. Cube removed bread; set aside. Combine remaining ingredients except vegetables and spoon into center of loaf. Cover and chill for 24 hours. Serve with reserved bread cubes and vegetables. Serves 8 to 10.

Give your home a spicy holiday scent year 'round. Cover oranges with whole cloves, piercing the peels in circle and swirl designs or simply covering the fruit at random. Roll in cinnamon and ginger, then stack in a wooden bowl.

Dill Pickle Dip

Pat Beach
Fisherville, KY

I fell in love with this recipe the first time I tried it at a wedding shower years ago. You're going to enjoy the unique salty-tart flavor.

8-oz. pkg. cream cheese,
   softened
2 c. sour cream
5 to 6 whole dill pickles,
   chopped

1-1/4 t. garlic salt, or to taste
Optional: pickle juice
potato chips

Mix together all ingredients except chips. If using, stir in pickle juice to desired consistency. Cover and chill 24 hours. Serve with chips. Serves 6 to 8.

Holly tortilla crisps…use a holly-shaped cookie cutter to cut out spinach tortillas. Bake at 350 degrees on an ungreased baking sheet for 7 minutes, or until crisp. Serve with your favorite dip or salsa.

Cheese-Olive Hot Snacks

Bonnie Studler
Los Angeles, CA

My sister and I make these snacks as part of our Christmas Eve dinner celebration. Their cheesy goodness and surprise green olive center make them a popular appetizer anytime.

5-oz. jar sharp pasteurized
   process cheese spread
1/4 c. butter, softened
1/8 t. hot pepper sauce
1/8 t. Worcestershire sauce

2/3 to 3/4 c. all-purpose flour
5-3/4 oz. jar green olives with
   pimentos, drained
1/4 t. pepper

In a bowl, blend cheese and butter until fluffy; add hot pepper and Worcestershire sauces, mixing well. Stir in enough flour to reach a dough consistency. Wrap each olive with a small piece of dough; roll so the olive is completely covered. Place on ungreased baking sheets. Bake at 400 degrees for 10 to 12 minutes, until lightly golden. Makes 15 to 20 servings.

When I was eight years old, my grandmother came to live with us. One December day, I came home from school and our tree was decorated with special memories from the past. My grandmother told my sisters and me that there was something special in the tree and we needed to look very hard. Four small boxes were hidden in different branches with our names on them. In my box were Cinderella's glass slipper necklace with the earrings to match. That was the best day of my life! My grandmother had made Christmas so special. I still have my necklace which I will treasure forever.

-Melissa Wolford, Fenton, MI

Bacon-Cheddar Appetizers

Annette Ingram
Grand Rapids, MI

We just adore these delicious bites of cheesy bacon-y goodness!
Fast and fun...a wonderful addition to your holiday spread!

8-oz. pkg. finely shredded sharp
   Cheddar cheese
1/2 c. mayonnaise
3 T. onion, finely chopped

1/2 c. bacon bits
64 shredded wheat crackers
Garnish: chopped red and green
   peppers

Mix together all ingredients except crackers and garnish until well
blended. Place crackers on lightly greased baking sheets. Top each
cracker with about one teaspoon of cheese mixture. Broil for
2 minutes, or until cheese is melted. Garnish with chopped peppers.
Makes about 5 dozen.

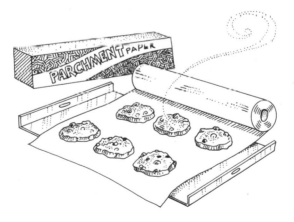

Instead of lightly greasing baking sheets, simply line them
with parchment paper cut to fit...there's no sticking
and clean-up is oh-so easy.

Honey-Glazed Snack Mix

Nancy Wise
Little Rock, AR

I love to whip up a batch of this yummy snack mix, place it in treat bags and affix it to my grandkids' presents. Such a pretty garnish, and the kids sure love it!

8 c. corn & rice cereal
3 c. mini pretzel twists
2 c. pecan halves

2/3 c. butter
1/2 c. honey

In a large bowl, combine cereal, pretzels and pecans; set aside. In a small saucepan over medium-low heat, melt butter. Stir in honey until well blended. Pour over cereal mixture; stir to coat. Spread into 2 greased 15"x10" jelly-roll pans. Bake at 350 degrees for 12 to 15 minutes, until mixture is lightly glazed, stirring occasionally. Cool for 3 minutes in pans; spread onto wax paper to cool completely. Store in an airtight container. Makes 13 cups.

Using recycled jars for holiday gift foods like Honey-Glazed Snack Mix? Remove stubborn labels and inked expiration dates with a swab of rubbing alcohol.

Glazed Walnuts

Brenda Huey
Geneva, IN

These are terrific to snack on and have around for the holidays. Scoop into jars and add a pretty ribbon for gifts. Sooo good!

1 c. maple syrup
1 T. butter
2 t. cinnamon

1/2 t. salt
1 t. vanilla extract
2 c. walnuts

In a cast-iron skillet over medium-low heat, cook syrup, butter, cinnamon and salt until thick. Remove from heat; stir in vanilla and walnuts until well coated. Transfer to baking sheets lined with wax paper to cool. Store in an airtight container. Makes 2 cups.

Craft a yo-yo wreath to share with girlfriends...you can make bunches in no time at all. Simply glue fabric yo-yos to a ring form and let dry.

Stuffed Mushrooms

Linda Harris
Colorado Springs, CO

I received this recipe from a friend many years ago. They are
a cinch to make and a family favorite at holiday parties. Be prepared
to share the recipe...they are delicious!

1 lb. sage-flavored ground pork
   sausage
8-oz. pkg. cream cheese,
   softened

25 to 30 small whole button
   mushrooms, stems removed

Brown sausage in a skillet over medium-high heat; drain. Transfer
to a bowl and combine with cream cheese, using a fork to blend
thoroughly. Place a rounded teaspoonful of sausage mixture inside
each mushroom cap. Place on lightly greased baking sheets. Bake at
350 degrees for 20 to 25 minutes, until heated through. Makes about
2-1/2 dozen.

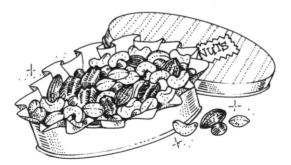

Having an informal party during the holidays? Keep it
simple...make one or two easy dishes and just pick up tasty
go-withs like deli salads, pickles, snack crackers and
cocktail nuts at a neighborhood grocery store.

Shrimp Puffs

Tiffani Schulte
Wyandotte, MI

My mom has been making this oh-so-simple appetizer since I was a kid. It has that kind of easy '70s feel about it, but I have never tried to update it in any way...it's just too good the way it is!

1 c. shredded Cheddar cheese
1 c. mayonnaise
6-oz. can small shrimp, drained
1/8 to 1/4 t. onion salt

12-oz. pkg. English muffins, split in half and cut into quarters

Mix together cheese, mayonnaise, shrimp and onion salt in a large bowl. Spread cheese mixture evenly across quartered English muffins. Place on aluminum-foil lined baking sheets. Bake at 350 degrees for 10 to 20 minutes, until cheese is melted and puffs are golden. Makes 4 to 5 dozen.

Pull out holiday and winter-themed stamp sets
and let the little ones decorate paper napkins to use
throughout the season!

Holiday Freezer Cheese Balls

Eileen Magiera
Milford, IN

*Made ahead, these cheese balls are perfect for
unexpected guests or to take to a party.*

1 c. shredded Cheddar cheese
1 c. pasteurized process cheese
  spread, shredded
2 8-oz. pkgs. cream cheese,
  softened
1.35-oz. pkg. onion soup mix
1/8 t. garlic powder
2 t. Worcestershire sauce
1/2 c. mayonnaise-style salad
  dressing
1/3 c. sugar
Garnish: chopped walnuts
assorted crackers

Place Cheddar cheese and cheese spread in a bowl and let stand at
room temperature for 2 hours. In a separate bowl, whip cream cheese
until smooth; blend in cheeses and remaining ingredients except
walnuts and crackers. Cover and refrigerate for one hour. Wet your
hands and form cheese mixture into 4 baseball-size balls. Roll each
in chopped walnuts to cover. Freeze each ball separately in plastic
zipping freezer bags. When ready to serve, remove to thaw completely
and serve with crackers. Makes 4 balls.

Celebrate the signs of winter in your entryway. Adorn
a parson's bench or small table with evergreen boughs
filled with items from the hobby store...doll-size sleds,
skates, mittens and scarves are just right!

Snacks & Appetizers

Christmas Cheese Log

Jan Phillips
Leola, PA

*We enjoy this creamy spread at our house on Christmas Eve afternoon
as we finish wrapping the last few presents.*

1/4 c. chopped pecans
8-oz. pkg. light cream cheese,
  softened
1/3 c. green onions, chopped
1 t. mustard
1 clove garlic, minced

1/4 t. hot pepper sauce
1 c. shredded sharp Cheddar
  cheese
1/4 c. fresh parsley, finely
  chopped
assorted crackers

Place pecans on an ungreased baking sheet. Bake at 350 degrees
for 8 minutes, stirring twice; let cool. Place cream cheese, onions,
mustard, garlic and hot pepper sauce in a bowl. Beat with an electric
mixer on slow speed for about 3 minutes. Stir in Cheddar cheese.
Shape into a log and wrap in plastic wrap. Chill for 15 to 20 minutes.
Mix parsley with toasted pecans and spread on a baking sheet or wax
paper. Unwrap log and roll in parsley mixture, covering completely.
Wrap again in plastic wrap and store in refrigerator until ready to
serve. Serve with crackers. Serves 6 to 8.

Have an appetizer swap with three or four girlfriends!
Each makes a big batch of her favorite dip, spread or finger food,
then get together to sample and divide 'em up. You'll all have
a super variety of goodies for holiday parties.

Creamy Artichoke Spread

JoAnn

*Delicious and oh-so pretty served in my favorite
ruby red glass serving bowl!*

14-oz. can artichoke hearts,
   drained and squeezed dry
1/2 c. mayonnaise
1/4 c. grated Parmesan cheese

1 clove garlic, minced
Garnish: paprika
assorted crackers

In a bowl, mash artichokes. Stir in mayonnaise, cheese and garlic.
Cover and chill. At serving time, sprinkle with paprika. Serve with
crackers. Serves 6.

As a girl, each Christmas I received a doll, but my special
memory revolves around the Christmas when I was in third
grade. I received a doll but there, under the tree, was something
I had never asked for or seen before. At our local hardware store,
my father had spotted a tin schoolhouse with all of the
accessories...a teacher, her students with their desks, a
blackboard and several other figurines. I was ecstatic! It was such
a wonderful surprise. Now, almost fifty years later, I still have
the schoolhouse and some of the accessories and I get the same
feeling when I look at them. Even though I don't recall the kind
of doll I received or the color of my pajamas, I will never forget
that Christmas and the schoolhouse Dad thought I needed.

-Connie Saunders, Hillsboro, KY

Mexican Pinwheels

Betsy Arnold
Dallas, OR

This is my daughter Katy's favorite quick
appetizer recipe...everyone loves it!

8-oz. container sour cream
8-oz. pkg. cream cheese,
  softened
4-oz. can diced green chiles,
  drained
4-oz. can chopped black olives,
  drained

1 c. finely shredded Mexican
  4-cheese blend
1 T. taco seasoning mix
6 10-inch flour tortillas
Garnish: salsa

Using an electric mixer on low speed, thoroughly blend all ingredients
except tortillas and salsa. Spread sour cream mixture evenly over
tortillas; roll up tortillas. Wrap each tightly in plastic wrap; refrigerate
for 3 to 4 hours. Remove plastic wrap; trim and discard ends. Cut
tortillas in 1/2 to 3/4-inch thick slices. Lay pinwheels flat on a serving
plate, leaving space in the center for a small bowl of salsa. Makes
about 4 dozen.

Make a snowman kit for your favorite kids! Just fill a
decorated box with lots of flea-market finds...a hat, large
buttons, a flannel scarf, mittens, twigs and an old corncob
pipe. All the kids have to add is snow and a carrot nose!

Peanut Butter Popcorn

Amy Teets
O'Fallon, MO

This recipe was handed down from a friend of the family. If you like, when you're done mixing, bake the popcorn on an ungreased baking sheet at 200 degrees for 20 minutes.

2 3-1/2 oz. pkgs. microwave
   popcorn, popped
1/2 c. margarine

3/4 c. brown sugar, packed
20 marshmallows
1/4 c. creamy peanut butter

Place popcorn into a large bowl; set aside. In a separate microwave-safe bowl, combine margarine, brown sugar and marshmallows. Microwave on high at one-minute intervals, stirring between each interval, until mixture is melted and smooth. Stir in peanut butter until well blended. Pour margarine mixture over popcorn; stir quickly to coat before it cools. Serves 8.

There's nothing like an invitation to share a cold winter afternoon with friends. It's fun to spend a lazy day playing board games and watching old movies. Take along a big bowl of Peanut Butter Popcorn to share.

Holiday Pretzel Rods

Louise Beveridge
Phillipsburg, PA

Roll the rods in colored sprinkles to match any holiday throughout the year. When December arrives, use red and green for Christmas and blue and white for Hanukkah. A tall mug or plastic cup is perfect for melting the coating.

1-1/2 c. semi-sweet chocolate chips
1/2 c. creamy peanut butter

10-oz. pkg. large pretzel rods
Garnish: chopped walnuts, chocolate or colored sprinkles

Microwave chocolate chips in a tall, narrow, microwave-safe container on high until melted, about 1-1/2 minutes. Add peanut butter and stir until combined. One at a time, dip pretzel rods two-thirds of the way into chocolate mixture; gently tap against side of container to remove excess. Immediately roll rod in desired garnish. Place on baking sheets lined with wax paper; let stand until completely set. Makes about 2-1/2 dozen.

Make a chocoholic gift basket! Fill it with gourmet cocoa, chocolate-dipped peppermint sticks and pretzels, chewy brownies, double chocolate cookies and cocoa-dusted truffles...a chocolate lover's dream!

Spinach-Parmesan Balls

Leah Dodson
Covington, KY

I made this appetizer for a Christmas gathering and it was a huge hit. Even the young children who were there wanted their mom to make it for them!

16-oz. pkg. frozen chopped
   spinach, thawed and drained
5 eggs, beaten
1 onion, minced
2 cloves garlic, minced
3/4 c. margarine, melted

1 c. shredded Parmesan cheese
1/2 t. dried thyme
1/2 t. cayenne pepper
1-3/4 c. Italian-style dry bread
   crumbs

Place spinach in a large bowl. Add remaining ingredients; mix well by hand. Shape into one-inch balls. Place closely together on lightly greased baking sheets. Bake at 350 degrees for 25 minutes. Makes 2-1/2 to 3-1/2 dozen.

When whisking together ingredients in a bowl, a damp kitchen towel can keep the bowl in place. Just twist the towel securely around the base of the bowl.

Favorite Spinach Bars

Kelly Patrick
Ashburn, VA

My mother got this recipe from one of her friends when I was just a child. It's a tried & true staple at the annual cookie exchange Mom and I have at her house. It has been passed on to family members, friends and co-workers. Even my brother, who is definitely not a spinach fan, absolutely loves it! It brings back so many memories of holiday gatherings, get-togethers with friends and recipe exchanges at work. I still have my original recipe card, with its food spatters, creases and all.

1/4 c. butter
2 10-oz. pkgs. frozen chopped
   spinach, thawed and drained
3 eggs, beaten
1 c. all-purpose flour
1 c. milk
1 t. paprika
16-oz. pkg. shredded Monterey
   Jack cheese
salt and pepper to taste

Melt butter in a 13"x9" baking pan set in a 350-degree oven. In a bowl, mix together remaining ingredients. Pour spinach mixture into pan. Bake at 350 degrees for 35 minutes. Cool for 10 minutes. Cut into bars to serve. Makes 16.

A kid-friendly appetizer! Serve chicken nuggets with this easy dipping sauce. Combine 1/3 cup catsup, 2 tablespoons maple syrup, 1/2 teaspoon Worcestershire sauce and 1/2 teaspoon soy sauce...yum!

Warm Welcome Reuben Dip

Bridget Jennings
Marquette, MI

My grandmother used to have Christmas Eve every year. Family &
friends gathered for games and appetizers after caroling or looking at
Christmas lights in town. This recipe reminds me of those times. Even
though my grandma has now passed on, we keep with tradition and
hold a Christmas Eve gathering where everyone is welcome.

1 c. shredded Swiss cheese
3 2-oz. pkgs. sliced corned beef,
   finely chopped
2 c. sauerkraut, drained and
   chopped

16-oz. bottle Thousand Island
   salad dressing
tortilla chips or round buttery
   crackers

In a bowl, mix together all ingredients except chips and crackers.
Transfer to a lightly greased 8"x8" baking pan. Bake, uncovered, at
350 degrees for 30 minutes, or until dip is heated through. Serve with
tortilla chips or crackers. Makes 2 dozen servings.

Just a dab of hot glue, some ribbon and vintage baubles can
transform ordinary silverware into something extraordinary.

Soups, Sides & Salads

Soup Supper

Old-Fashioned Mashed Potatoes

Hannah King
Cleveland, TN

These mashed potatoes are always requested for holidays and special gatherings. They're buttery, creamy and delicious! Your whole family will enjoy them.

5 lbs. yellow potatoes, peeled
   and cut into large cubes
1 c. butter, softened

12-oz. can evaporated milk
salt and pepper to taste

Place potatoes in a large stockpot. Add water to cover. Bring to a simmer and cook over medium-high heat for 20 to 25 minutes, until tender. Remove from heat and drain. Place potatoes back into stockpot; add butter. Mash with a potato masher or hand mixer. Add evaporated milk and stir until well combined. Add salt and pepper to taste. Serves 8 to 12.

Tasty Potatoes

Peggy Dannehl
Grand Island, NE

Whenever I take these potatoes to gatherings, I always come home with an empty dish and requests for the recipe. Now my kids are making them for their families. I think it's the cream of onion soup that makes them so tasty.

Optional: 1/2 c. white onion,
   chopped
Optional: 2 T. butter, softened
10-3/4 oz. can cream of onion
   soup

1 c. shredded Cheddar cheese,
   divided
8-oz. container sour cream
12-oz. pkg. frozen shredded
   hashbrowns

In a skillet over medium heat, sauté onion in butter, if desired. Stir in soup, 3/4 cup cheese, sour cream and hashbrowns. Pour into a greased 8"x8" baking pan. Top with remaining cheese. Bake, uncovered, at 350 degrees for 30 to 45 minutes, until cheese is melted. Makes 8 servings.

Soups, Sides & Salads

Dad's Fried Stuffing

Kristina Trice
Frederick, MD

The one reason everyone comes to our house for the holidays...my dad's stuffing. Be sure you make extra for leftovers!

1-lb. loaf bread, torn into
   bite-size pieces
1 c. butter
1 onion, diced

3 stalks celery, diced
1 to 1-1/2 c. milk
2 eggs, beaten
salt and pepper to taste

Place bread into a large bowl. Melt butter in a large skillet over medium heat; sauté onion and celery until tender. In a separate bowl, beat together one cup milk and eggs. Add salt and pepper. Pour milk mixture over bread; toss to coat. All the bread should be moist; if not, add remaining milk. Mix with your hands; transfer to skillet with onion mixture. Fry until golden and crispy. Makes 8 to 10 servings.

Every Christmas Eve as they were growing up, we measured
our children and marked their heights on the door frame so
Santa would leave the right size if they got clothes. It was so fun
to have everyone line up and be marked on the chart with
excitement and wonder at what Santa would bring! Now they
are older and Santa doesn't bring them presents, but oh, when
they line up at the door, for just a minute there is magic.

-Marie Freiberger, Bowdoinham, ME

Yorkshire Pudding

Margaret Hoehler
Littleton, CO

An old recipe from my mother-in-law. This is especially good when the pan is greased with drippings from roast beef.

1-1/2 c. all-purpose flour
3/4 t. salt
1-1/2 c. milk

3 eggs, beaten
1/2 c. currants

Mix together flour, salt, milk and eggs in a bowl. Beat well with a wire whisk. Fold in currants. Pour into a greased 8"x8" baking pan. Bake, uncovered, at 450 degrees for 25 to 30 minutes. Makes 6 to 8 servings.

A pretty way to dress up the dining room! Use clothespins to clip holiday cards on a ribbon and tie onto chair backs, the sideboard edge or a china cabinet shelf.

Carrot Pudding

Bonnie Zarch
Skokie, IL

*My mother used to make this side dish for family holiday dinners
in our metal gelatin mold pan. After inverting on a large platter,
she put peas in the middle for a colorful look.*

3 16-oz. pkgs. frozen sliced
   carrots
6 eggs, separated
1-1/2 c. all-purpose flour
1 t. salt

1-1/2 t. cream of tartar
1-1/2 t. baking soda
3/4 c. brown sugar, packed
3/4 c. margarine, softened

Prepare carrots according to package directions; drain and set aside. In
a bowl, beat egg whites until stiff peaks form. In a separate bowl, sift
together flour, salt, cream of tartar and baking soda. In another bowl,
blend together brown sugar and margarine. Beat egg yolks until light.
Alternately add egg yolks and flour mixture to brown sugar mixture.
Add carrots, mashing well. Fold in egg whites. Place in a greased
12"x9" baking pan. Bake, uncovered, at 350 degrees for 40 minutes.
Makes 8 servings.

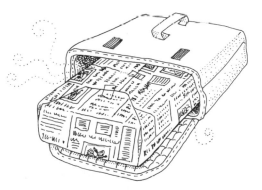

If you're taking a casserole to a holiday party, keep it toasty
by covering the casserole dish with aluminum foil, then
wrapping it in several layers of newspaper or even gift wrap!

Grandma Baker's Soup

Peggy Piatt
Columbia, MO

My dad didn't like all the vegetables in vegetable soup, so my grandma made this recipe. Since she knew how much I loved it, she would call me and say, "I have a bowl of Grandma Baker's Soup ready for you!" We now make this every Christmas. The longer it cooks, the better the flavor.

2 lbs. ground beef
1 onion, chopped
5 lbs. potatoes, cut into
   bite-sized pieces

2 16-oz. cans diced tomatoes
6 c. water
salt and pepper to taste

In a Dutch oven over medium heat, brown ground beef and onion; drain. Add remaining ingredients. Bring to a boil; reduce heat to low. Cover and simmer, stirring occasionally, for one to 2 hours. Makes 7 to 8 servings.

Super-special bread to go with this soup! Cut a loaf of
French bread into slices, stopping just short of the bottom crust.
Combine 3/4 cup shredded Cheddar cheese, 1/2 cup butter,
1/4 cup chopped fresh parsley, one teaspoon paprika and 3 to
4 cloves minced garlic and then spread mixture between slices.
Wrap up in aluminum foil and heat in a 350-degree oven
for about 15 minutes. Tasty!

Beckie's Garlic Soup

Beckie Butcher
Elgin, IL

*I invented this soup recipe on a cold Chicago afternoon. The last thing
I wanted to do was leave the house, so I went through my refrigerator
and my lazy Susan instead...this is the delicious result!*

1/4 c. butter	14-1/2 oz. can chicken broth
3 cloves garlic, minced	2 T. grated Parmesan cheese
1 onion, chopped	1-1/2 t. dried parsley
12-oz. can evaporated milk	1/4 t. cayenne pepper

In a skillet over medium heat, melt butter; sauté garlic and onion until
tender. Add remaining ingredients and bring to a boil. Reduce heat
and let simmer for 10 to 15 minutes, stirring occasionally.
Serves 4.

A favorite cook will love receiving a gift of a soup "kit." Fill a
red-speckled enamelware soup pot with soup bowls, oversized
table napkins and a soup ladle...toss in a package of mini
alphabet noodles, just for fun.

Roasted Green Beans

Tara Horton
Gooseberry Patch

These ingredients are always in my kitchen...I use fresh green beans in the summer and frozen in the winter. Toss in two tablespoons of slivered almonds if you want to be fancy!

1-1/4 lbs. green beans
1 T. lemon juice
2 t. olive oil
1/4 t. garlic powder

1/4 t. dried basil
1/2 t. salt
1/4 t. pepper

Toss together all ingredients on an ungreased 15"x10" jelly-roll pan. Bake at 450 degrees for 10 minutes, or until tender. Serves 4 to 6.

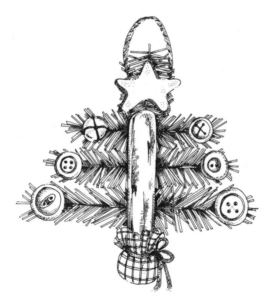

Pull out your button box for oodles of holiday inspiration!
Stitch buttons on mitten cuffs or the ends of woolly scarves.
You can add several to the edges of a tablecloth or
string them together for a country-style garland.

Roasted Brussels Sprouts
with Pancetta

Denise Piccirilli
Huber Heights, OH

This just happens to be a newer and easier version of an older recipe.
Canadian bacon can be substituted for the pancetta, if you prefer.

2 lbs. Brussels sprouts, sliced
    in half
6-oz. pkg. pancetta, chopped

1/4 c. olive oil
kosher salt and pepper to taste

In a large bowl, combine Brussels sprouts, pancetta and oil. Toss well
to coat; season with salt and pepper. Spread mixture in one layer on
an ungreased 15"x10" jelly-roll pan. Bake at 425 degrees for 25 to
30 minutes, until Brussels sprouts are crisp-tender. Serves 4 to 6.

For centuries men have kept an appointment
with Christmas. Christmas means
fellowship, feasting, giving and receiving,
a time of good cheer, home.

-W.J. Tucker

Penne with Kale & Onion

Sandra Sullivan
Aurora, CO

*We didn't think we liked kale until I swapped it for the spinach in
this yummy recipe. But you can always use spinach if you wish.*

1 onion, sliced
2 T. olive oil, divided
8 cloves garlic, thinly sliced

3 c. penne pasta, uncooked
6 c. kale, chopped
1/2 t. salt

In a large skillet over medium heat, cook onion in one tablespoon
oil for 15 to 20 minutes, or until golden. Add garlic during the last
2 minutes of cook time. In a large stockpot filled with boiling water,
cook pasta according to package directions; drain and drizzle with
remaining oil. In a Dutch oven, bring one inch of water to a boil and
add kale. Cover and cook for 10 to 15 minutes, until tender; drain.
Stir salt, pasta and kale into onion mixture and heat through. Makes
6 servings.

Creamy Noodles

Tara Geiger
Carrollton, TX

*This comforting dish of my grandmother's is so easy...one of the first
I learned how to make.*

4 14-1/2 oz. cans chicken broth
12-oz. can evaporated milk
1/2 c. butter

16-oz. pkg. extra wide egg
noodles, uncooked

Bring broth and milk to a boil in a large stockpot over medium
heat. Add butter and egg noodles. Cook until tender, about 10 to
15 minutes. Serves 8.

Walnut-Parsley Pesto Linguine

Regina Wickline
Pebble Beach, CA

The walnut and parsley in this terrific dish really complement each other. So versatile too...I have stirred in thinly sliced, cooked portabella mushrooms and sun-dried tomatoes as well as steamed green beans or asparagus before. You can even serve it chilled as a pasta salad! Yum!

16 oz. pkg. linguine pasta,
   uncooked
2 c. fresh flat-leaf parsley,
   coarsely chopped
1 c. chopped walnuts, toasted
3/4 c. shredded Parmigiano-
   Reggiano cheese
1 c. green onions, thinly sliced

1 t. salt
1/2 c. olive oil
2 to 3 t. lemon juice
3 to 4 T. water
pepper to taste
Garnish: grated Parmesan
   cheese

Cook pasta according to package directions; drain. Meanwhile, place parsley, walnuts, cheese, onions and salt in a food processor. Process ingredients while slowly pouring in olive oil until mixture forms a thick paste. Continue to process while slowly adding lemon juice and water to thin mixture to a smooth consistency. Toss with warm linguine and garnish with Parmesan cheese; serve immediately. Makes 4 to 6 servings.

A fun countdown to Christmas! Get the family together during dinner and think up twenty-five fun holiday activities like making gingerbread cookies for classmates, dancing to holiday music, sledding or reading a Christmas story. Write each on a paper strip, link them together and then pull one off each day in December and do the activity together.

Turnip Mashed Potatoes

Cindy McKinnon
El Dorado, AR

A wonderfully creamy dish. My family loves when I make it!

6 redskin potatoes, peeled and
    sliced 1/4-inch thick
2 turnips, peeled and sliced
    1/4-inch thick

1/2 c. milk, heated
1/2 c. butter, melted
1/2 c. sour cream
salt and pepper to taste

Place potatoes and turnips in a stockpot filled with boiling water; boil for 15 minutes, or until crisp-tender. Drain. Whip potatoes and turnips with an electric mixer, mixing until moderately smooth. Add hot milk, butter and sour cream. Season with salt and pepper. Whip again until well blended. Serves 4 to 6.

Oven-Fried Potatoes

Tina Dillon
Parma, OH

These "fries" have a terrific flavor and go well with
meatloaf...or just catsup!

8 potatoes, cut into wedges
1/2 c. oil
2 T. grated Parmesan cheese

1 t. salt
1/2 t. paprika
1/2 t. garlic powder

Arrange potato wedges, skin-side down, in an ungreased 15"x10" jelly-roll pan. In a bowl, whisk together remaining ingredients; brush over potatoes. Bake at 375 degrees for 45 minutes. Makes 6 to 8 servings.

Baked Cauliflower

Amy Gitter
Omro, WI

My mom passed this holiday meal recipe on to our families.
It's so good, even the kids love it!

1 head cauliflower, cut into
   bite-size pieces
1 c. dry bread crumbs
1/2 c. grated Parmesan cheese
1/8 t. salt

1/8 t. pepper
1/8 t. onion salt
1/4 t. garlic, minced
1/2 c. butter, melted

Place cauliflower in a large stockpot filled with boiling, salted water. Boil for about 6 minutes, or until tender. Drain cauliflower and spoon into a greased 1-1/2 quart casserole dish. Combine remaining ingredients except butter and sprinkle over cauliflower. Drizzle melted butter over top. Bake, uncovered, at 350 degrees for 30 minutes, or until golden. Serves 12.

To keep cauliflower fresh and creamy white,
add a tablespoon of milk to the water
when steaming or boiling.

Souper Rice

Sue Coppersmith
Granbury, TX

A potluck favorite and tasty comfort food. Add two cups of cubed, cooked chicken to make a "souper" main dish.

8-oz. can chopped green chiles
3 c. cooked rice
1 c. sour cream
10-3/4 oz. can cream of celery
   soup

salt and pepper to taste
3/4 c. shredded Colby-Jack
   cheese

Mix together undrained chiles, rice, sour cream, soup and seasonings. Spoon into an 11"x9" baking pan that has been sprayed with non-stick vegetable spray. Sprinkle cheese on top. Bake, uncovered, at 350 degrees for 25 to 30 minutes, until bubbly. Serves 8 to 10.

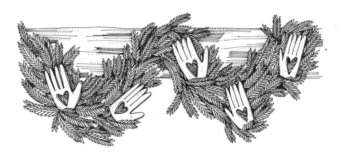

Make and give this tasty Herb Dip Mix. In a plastic zipping bag, combine 1-1/2 tablespoons dried parsley, 1-1/2 tablespoons dried, minced onion, 1/4 teaspoon dill weed, 1/2 teaspoon salt and 1/2 teaspoon seasoning salt. Directions: Mix one cup sour cream with one cup of mayonnaise. Stir in Herb Dip Mix. Cover and chill for one hour.

Merry Christmas Rice

Kerry Mayer
Dunham Springs, LA

Each year, the women in our family gather together to prepare a Christmas feast. My oldest daughter Kim just turned fifteen and got to help this year. This quick & easy recipe with festive red and green peppers was her very first dish on the holiday table. It turned out great...I am so proud of her! This can easily be doubled or tripled to feed a crowd.

1/2 c. onion, finely chopped
3 stalks celery, finely chopped
1/2 red pepper, chopped
1/2 green pepper, chopped
1 T. butter, softened

2 c. chicken broth
2 c. instant rice, uncooked
Optional: 1/2 t. salt
1/4 t. pepper

In a skillet over medium heat, sauté onion, celery and peppers in butter for 2 minutes, or until crisp-tender. Remove from heat; set aside. In a saucepan over medium-high heat, bring broth to a full boil. Remove from heat. Quickly stir in rice, onion mixture, salt if desired and pepper. Cover and let stand for 6 to 7 minutes. Stir before serving. Serves 6.

It's easy to turn a vintage painted metal tray into a whimsical wall clock with a clock kit from your local craft store. Drill a center hole, then insert the clock movement and hands. Press on self-adhesive numbers...time's up!

Cranberry Salad

Gwen Hudson
Madison Heights, VA

*My mother made this gelatin salad every Christmas when
I was growing up, but it's a hit any time of year.*

2 16-oz. pkgs. cranberries	2 1-oz. envs. unflavored gelatin
2 oranges, peeled, sectioned and seeds removed	1 c. hot water
	1 c. celery, diced
2 c. sugar	1 c. chopped nuts

Process cranberries in a food processor until finely ground; set aside.
Repeat processing with oranges. In a large bowl, stir sugar and gelatin
in hot water to dissolve; let cool. Add cranberries, oranges, celery and
nuts; mix well. Cover and refrigerate until set. Serves 8 to 10.

Waxed dental floss is super for stringing old-fashioned
garlands of cranberries and popcorn. It's stronger than
regular thread and the waxed coating slides right through!

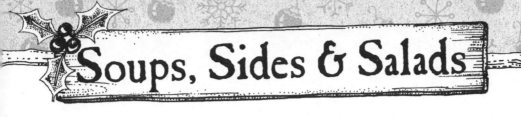
Frozen Cherry Salad

LaShelle Brown
Mulvane, KS

Around the holidays, my Grandpa Don always asked my mom to make this salad. It almost tastes like cherry ice cream...yummy!

21-oz. can cherry pie filling
14-oz. can sweetened
  condensed milk

8-oz. container frozen whipped
  topping, thawed

In a medium serving bowl, mix together pie filling and condensed milk. Fold in whipped topping. Cover and freeze. Serves 10 to 12.

With houses decorated inside and out for the holidays, it's a perfect time to hold a progressive dinner! Each family serves one course at their house as everyone travels from home to home. Begin at one house for appetizers, move to the next for soups and salads, again for the main dish and end with dessert. It's all about food & fun!

Mimie's Christmas Apple & Chicken Salad

Beckie Apple
Grannis, AR

As a child I always looked forward to the special foods we only had at the holiday meal. This recipe of my Mimie's is one of my favorites!

2 c. cooked chicken breast, finely chopped
4 red apples, peeled, cored and chopped
2 c. mini marshmallows
1/2 c. raisins

1/2 c. pecans, finely chopped
2 T. onion, minced
1/2 c. celery, finely diced
1/4 t. salt
1/2 c. mayonnaise

Toss together all ingredients except mayonnaise in a large bowl; mix well. Fold in mayonnaise; coat well. Cover and chill before serving. Serves 8.

Turn vintage jelly glasses into candles. Holding a wick in place, pour scented wax gel into each glass. They're especially pretty with gels in glowing "jelly" colors like red and amber!

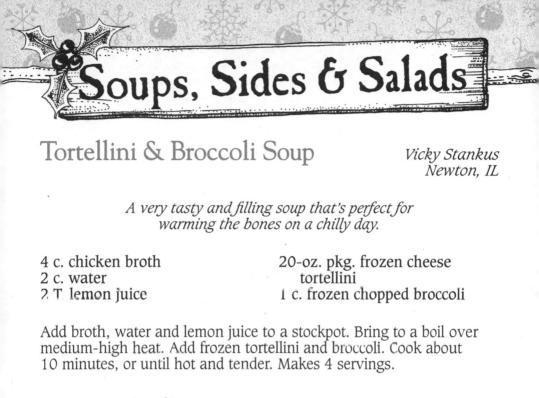

Soups, Sides & Salads

Tortellini & Broccoli Soup

Vicky Stankus
Newton, IL

A very tasty and filling soup that's perfect for
warming the bones on a chilly day.

4 c. chicken broth
2 c. water
2 T. lemon juice

20-oz. pkg. frozen cheese
   tortellini
1 c. frozen chopped broccoli

Add broth, water and lemon juice to a stockpot. Bring to a boil over medium-high heat. Add frozen tortellini and broccoli. Cook about 10 minutes, or until hot and tender. Makes 4 servings.

Cheesy Hashbrown Potato Soup

Joyce Stearns
Murphysboro, IL

We enjoy this delicious soup at our annual
Christmas ornament party.

28-oz. pkg. frozen diced
   potatoes with onions and
   peppers
14-1/2 oz. can chicken broth

salt and pepper to taste
8-oz. pkg. pasteurized process
   cheese spread, cubed

Place frozen potatoes in a large stockpot. Add chicken broth and enough water to cover potatoes. Season with salt and pepper. Bring to a boil over medium-high heat and cook until potatoes are tender, about 8 minutes. Add cheese, stirring until cheese melts. Season with additional salt and pepper to taste if needed. Serves 6.

Ms. Margaret's Biscuits

Lisa Cox
Spottsville, KY

A dear lady, Ms. Margaret, lived next to us when I was growing up. Even though my family moved, we always kept in touch. She shared this recipe with me during a Christmas visit after my daughter Breeanna was born. Ms. Margaret passed away this last year, but I will always remember her and the memories we shared when I make Ms. Margaret's Biscuits!

1 c. sour cream
1 c. self-rising flour

1/2 c. butter, softened

Mix all ingredients together well. Fill lightly greased mini muffin cups 2/3 full with dough. Bake at 425 degrees for 15 minutes. Makes 2 dozen.

Tie up a present with a fun jump rope.
It keeps the package snug and doubles as a gift!

Easy Cheesy Orzo

Lori Jones
Ottawa, KS

Everyone who tries this wants the recipe...it's so easy & yummy!

2 T. olive oil
1/2 onion, chopped
2 cloves garlic, chopped
2 14 1/2 oz. cans chicken broth

2 c. orzo pasta, uncooked
1/2 c. grated Parmigiano-
   Reggiano cheese
salt and pepper to taste

Heat oil in a medium saucepan with a tight-fitting lid over medium heat. Add onion and garlic; sauté for 2 to 3 minutes. Add broth to pan and bring to a boil. Stir in orzo and return to a boil. Cover and reduce heat to a simmer. Cook 15 minutes, stirring occasionally, or until liquid is absorbed and orzo is tender. Remove lid and stir in cheese. Season with salt and pepper to taste. Makes 8 servings.

Two for one! Double a favorite side dish and freeze half.
Another night, turn the remaining portion into a main dish
by adding some meat to it. Salsa rice with cubed chicken,
baked beans with sliced sausage and macaroni & cheese
with diced ham are just a few creative ideas.

Macaroni & Cheese Twist

Mel Chencharick
Julian, PA

Either as a side or as the main dish, this little twist on traditional mac & cheese is fast and easy.

2 c. rotini pasta, uncooked
1/2 c. green pepper, diced
1 clove garlic, minced
1 T. oil
2 8-oz. cans tomato sauce
1 c. water

1/2 t. dried oregano
2 T. fresh parsley, finely
   chopped
1/2 c. finely shredded Cheddar
   cheese

Cook rotini according to package directions; drain. Meanwhile, in a skillet over medium heat, sauté pepper and garlic in oil just until tender. Add tomato sauce, water, oregano and parsley. Reduce heat and simmer for 10 minutes. Add cheese; stir to mix and melt the cheese. Place cooked pasta into a serving dish. Pour pepper mixture over pasta to serve. Serves 4 to 6.

Clever party favors! Remove the caps from clear glass ornaments, then write holiday greetings on pieces of paper no wider than the ornament. Roll up each greeting, tie with ribbon, slip inside the ornament and replace the cap.

Festive Broccoli Salad

Carol Shrum
Gastonia, NC

*This cold broccoli dish is super in the summer with burgers
or steaks and gorgeous to serve at Christmas in a
vintage crystal bowl from Grandma.*

2 heads broccoli, chopped into
   flowerets
1 red onion, chopped
1/2 to 3/4 c. sweetened dried
   cranberries

3-oz. jar bacon bits
1 c. mayonnaise
2 T. red wine vinegar
1/2 c. sugar

Mix together broccoli, onion, cranberries and bacon bits in a large
bowl. Whisk together remaining ingredients in a separate bowl and
pour over top of broccoli mixture, just before serving. Toss to mix.
Serves 8.

One of my favorite Christmas memories was when my
goddaughter Courtney and I made a snowman. My grandmother
lived just a few houses away. In her yard we found some stones
for the eyes and mouth and sticks for the arms and nose. In her
house we picked a scarf to put around the snowman's neck. We
built the snowman facing my grandmother's front door, making
it easy for her to just look out the front window and see the
snowman. Grandmother said the snowman reminded her of
when she was a child and built snowmen with her brothers.

-Carol Clendinnen, Coral Springs, FL

Seafood Pasta Salad

Kristy Mertes
Brownville, NE

This is my favorite pasta salad. Serve in footed bowls with a sprig of parsley on top for an elegant presentation.

2 c. spiral pasta, uncooked
1/2 c. mayonnaise-style salad dressing
1/4 c. Italian salad dressing
2 T. grated Parmesan cheese

8-oz. pkg. imitation crabmeat, chopped
1/4 c. green onion, chopped
1/2 c. green pepper, chopped
1/2 c. tomato, chopped

Cook pasta according to package directions; drain and rinse in cold water. Combine dressings and cheese in a bowl and mix well. Add pasta and remaining ingredients; mix lightly. Chill before serving. Serves 4.

Cheesy Ranch Dressing

Brenda Schlosser
Brighton, CO

Given to me by my aunt over thirty years ago, this dressing is best served on an iceberg lettuce salad with lots and lots of veggies. I like to add broccoli, carrot, red peppers, mushrooms, onion, radishes, cucumbers and crunchy croutons.

4 c. mayonnaise-type salad dressing
1 T. white vinegar
2 T. Worcestershire sauce
1 T. garlic salt

2 T. sugar
2/3 to 1 c. milk
1 c. Cheddar or blue cheese, grated

Combine all ingredients in a bowl or food processor. Refrigerate until ready to serve. Makes about 6-1/2 cups.

Sweet Potato Casserole

David Sopha
Odenton, MD

A classic holiday recipe! Boil three to four peeled sweet potatoes to make three cups of mashed.

3 c. sweet potatoes, cooked and mashed
1/2 c. sugar
2 eggs, beaten
1/3 c. evaporated milk

1/2 c. butter, melted, slightly cooled and divided
1 c. brown sugar, packed
1/3 c. all-purpose flour
1 c. pecans, coarsely chopped

Mix together sweet potatoes, sugar, eggs, milk and 1/4 cup butter. Spoon into a greased 13"x9" baking pan. Mix together remaining butter and other ingredients. Sprinkle over sweet potato mixture. Bake, uncovered, at 350 degrees for 35 to 40 minutes. Serves 8 to 10.

Instead of marshmallows, try topping a favorite sweet potato casserole recipe with canned, sliced peaches and cashews. Sure to be a hit!

Susan's Sweet Potatoes

Beth Folkeringa
Ontario, Canada

*My sister-in-law Susan used to serve these potatoes at
special events. She passed away a few years ago, but I make
this dish in her honor every holiday.*

4 sweet potatoes, cooked,
    peeled and mashed
2 eggs, beaten
1 t. vanilla extract
1/2 t. salt

1/2 c. butter, softened
1/2 to 3/4 c. brown sugar,
    packed
10-1/2 oz. pkg. mini
    marshmallows

Mix together all ingredients except marshmallows. Spread in a greased
13"x9" baking pan. Bake, uncovered, at 350 degrees for 15 minutes.
Remove from oven and cover top with marshmallows. Bake an
additional 15 minutes, or until marshmallows are lightly golden.
Serves 8 to 10.

A snow-covered wreath in a twinkle! Spray-paint pine cones
completely white. Use the same paint to lightly spray an
evergreen wreath, allowing some green needles to show
through. When dry, hot-glue pine cones to the
front of the wreath and tie on a red bow.

Easy Cheesy Chicken & Dumpling Soup

Stephanie Pearman
Vine Grove, KY

I first made this quick & easy soup as a new bride after a friend shared it with me. Seven years later my husband still requests it! I love making it in the fall the best. Break up the carrots a bit so the soup looks like it was made from scratch...hee-hee!

4 10-3/4 oz. cans cream of
   chicken soup
4 14-1/2-oz. cans chicken broth
1 c. milk
salt and pepper to taste
4 chicken breasts, cooked and
   shredded

1 c. shredded Cheddar cheese
2 14-1/2 oz. cans sliced carrots,
   drained
10-oz. tube refrigerated biscuits,
   quartered

In a large stockpot over medium-low heat, combine soup, broth and milk; mix well. Add seasonings, chicken and cheese; stir until cheese melts, about 10 minutes. Mix in carrots; top with biscuit pieces. Cover and simmer on low until biscuits are cooked through, about 20 minutes. Serves 8.

On a cozy tree-trimming night, if you're stringing
popcorn garlands, save some freshly popped corn
to enjoy as a fun soup topper.

Quick Cream of Chicken & Leek Soup

Laura Witham
Anchorage, AK

I was in a hurry, but serving plain cream of chicken soup out of the can was just not an option. So I dressed it up and everyone thought I spent hours in the kitchen making this delicious soup! It's definitely going to be my secret "go-to" recipe whenever I'm in a pinch again!

2 T. olive oil
2 boneless, skinless chicken
   breasts, diced
1 leek, diced
salt and pepper to taste

1-1/2 t. Italian seasoning
4 cloves garlic, minced
juice of 1 lime
2 10-3/4 oz. cans cream of
   chicken soup

Heat oil in a saucepan over medium-high heat. Add chicken and cook until golden. Add remaining ingredients except soup. Reduce heat to medium-low. Sauté until leek is tender, about 2 to 3 minutes. Stir in soup. Cover and simmer for 5 to 7 minutes. Serves 4.

Give frozen ready-to-bake dinner rolls a homemade touch.
Before baking, brush rolls with egg beaten with a little water.
Sprinkle with sesame seed or coarse salt and bake as usual.

Soups, Sides & Salads

Pickled Beets & Eggs

Bev Shealy
Worthington, OH

This yummy and pretty recipe was my mother's. She used a strainer as she poured the pickling liquid over the beets and eggs.

2 c. sugar
2 c. water
2 c. vinegar
1 T. cinnamon
1 t. ground cloves

1 t. allspice
1 t. salt
15-oz. can sliced beets, drained
6 eggs, hard-boiled, peeled and sliced

In a saucepan over medium heat, bring sugar, water, vinegar and spices to a boil. Place beets in a large bowl; top with eggs. Pour sugar mixture over top. Chill until serving time. Serves 6.

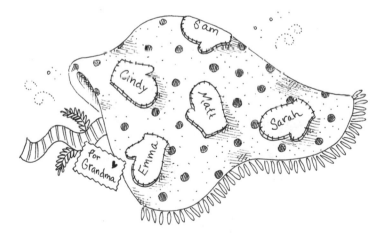

Stitch a cozy surprise for Grandma. Trim a
store-bought fleece throw with fleece mitten shapes
that have been embroidered with the
grandkids' names...so easy!

Dill Vegetable Salad

Liz Plotnick-Snay
Gooseberry Patch

*My mother in-law's original recipe for this dish was called
Dill Cucumber Salad, but we love it with tomatoes and onions!*

3 cucumbers, peeled and thinly
   sliced
1 pt. cherry tomatoes, halved
1/4 sweet onion, finely chopped
3/4 c. lemon juice

1/2 c. olive oil
3 T. honey
1 t. dill weed
1/2 t. garlic powder
1/8 t. salt

Place cucumbers, tomatoes and onion in a large bowl. In a separate
bowl, whisk together remaining ingredients; pour over cucumber
mixture. Toss to coat. Cover and refrigerate overnight. Serves
10 to 12.

Try a new side dish instead of rice or noodles...barley pilaf.
Simply prepare quick-cooking barley with chicken broth,
seasoned with a little chopped onion and dried parsley.
Filling, speedy and tasty!

Asparagus Casserole

Sheila Thompson Castellini
Raton, NM

We always had this rich-tasting dish for winter holidays when we couldn't get fresh vegetables. It wouldn't have been the holidays without it!

8-oz. pkg. frozen peas
8-oz. pkg. frozen cut asparagus
4-oz. can sliced water chestnuts, drained
1 c. pasteurized process cheese spread, diced
10-3/4 oz. can cream of mushroom soup
2.8-oz. can French fried onions, divided

In a bowl, mix together frozen vegetables, water chestnuts, cheese, soup and half the onions. Place in a lightly greased 8"x8" baking pan. Bake, uncovered, at 350 degrees for 25 minutes. Sprinkle with remaining onions; bake for an additional 5 minutes. Let stand for 5 minutes before serving. Serves 8 to 10.

Christmas is the perfect time to celebrate your heritage. Learn about holiday traditions of the countries in your family. Decorate the Christmas tree with matching colors from the countries' flags.

Eggplant & Tomato Casserole

Lisa Ashton
Aston, PA

Being fellow Italians, my co-worker friend and I loved sharing recipes with each other. This recipe of hers is a wonderful way to use the veggies from my garden.

1 onion, chopped
2 eggplants, peeled and diced
1/4 c. butter, softened
5 tomatoes, peeled, seeded and
   cut into chunks

1 t. salt
1/2 t. pepper
1/4 c. dry bread crumbs

Sauté onion and eggplants in butter in a skillet over medium heat until golden. Add tomatoes, salt and pepper; mix well. Spoon into a greased 1-1/2 quart casserole dish. Sprinkle bread crumbs over top. Bake, uncovered, at 350 degrees for 30 minutes. Makes 6 servings.

Dress up a plain canvas shopping tote for a sweet and useful gift...just stitch on rows and rows of colorful rick rack.

Comfort Corn Pudding

JoAnn

Mmm...a side dish that's just right alongside a casual supper of Sloppy Joes or a sit-down dinner of roast chicken.

2 14-3/4 oz. cans creamed corn
15-1/4 oz. can corn, drained
1 c. sour cream
1/2 c. butter, melted
8-1/2 oz. pkg. cornbread mix

In a bowl, mix together creamed corn, corn, sour cream and butter. Stir in dry cornbread mix; blend well. Pour into a 13"x9" baking pan that has been sprayed with non-stick vegetable spray. Bake, uncovered, at 375 degrees for 30 to 40 minutes, until a toothpick inserted into the center comes out clean. Serves 9.

Kids will gobble up this casserole when it's spooned into custard cups before baking. Easy to serve and just their size!

Broccoli Cornbread

Kimberly Mansell
Midland, TX

This is one of my holiday traditions. My kids will clean out the pan if I let them! My husband always asks me to bake it for his work parties.

2 8-1/2 oz. pkgs. cornbread
    mix
16-oz. container cream-style
    cottage cheese
2 eggs, beaten

1 onion, chopped
10-oz. pkg. frozen chopped
    broccoli, thawed
1/2 c. shredded Cheddar cheese

In a large bowl, blend dry cornbread mix, cottage cheese, eggs and onion; mix well. Fold in broccoli. Spoon into a greased 13"x9" glass baking pan. Bake, uncovered, at 350 degrees for 35 minutes, or until a toothpick comes out clean. While still warm, sprinkle with Cheddar cheese. Allow to cool before serving. Makes 12 to 15 servings.

After the last Christmas tree ornament is put away you can reuse the evergreen boughs. Cut off the branches and lay them over your garden perennials to provide protection during the cold weather.

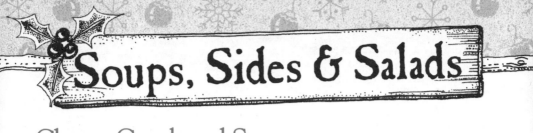

Cheesy Cornbread Soup

Diana Krol
Nickerson, KS

A quick recipe we enjoy, especially on a cold winter night!
Extra nice served with a fruit salad and good crusty bread.

1 c. onion, chopped
6 T. butter
8-1/2 oz. pkg. cornbread mix
2 14-1/2 oz. cans chicken broth
2 14-3/4 oz. cans creamed corn

1 c. shredded Cheddar cheese
2 c. whipping cream
Garnish: additional shredded
  Cheddar cheese

In a stockpot over medium heat, sauté onion in butter. Stir in dry cornbread mix. Stir in broth and corn until smooth. Fold in cheese; stir to melt. Just before serving, stir in cream; heat through but do not boil. Garnish with additional cheese. Serves 8.

Remember making paper snowflakes? Revive the tradition...fold white felt squares into fourths and cut into snowflake shapes. Use a paper punch to cut out shapes and stitch onto a stocking.

Rita's Wild Rice

Sharon Jones
Oklahoma City, OK

This is one of my mom's favorite recipes. It makes a fabulous side dish to anything! We have it with our special meals. Tastes even better the second day.

6-oz. pkg. long-grain and wild
   rice mix
1/2 c. onion, chopped
1/2 c. carrots, peeled and
   chopped

1/2 c. celery, chopped
1/2 c. radish, chopped
3/4 c. Italian salad dressing

Prepare rice according to package directions; let cool. Toss rice with chopped veggies. Stir in salad dressing to coat. Serve at room temperature or chilled. Serves 4 to 6.

A week after Thanksgiving, homeschooling was not going particularly smoothly. So, in a moment of inspiration I sent my sons TJ and Nathan to write out their Christmas lists. Penmanship practice was never so much fun! Stephen, just a little over four years old, thought he was in school too. So, he got a piece of paper and started printing away. After a short while he asked, "Mom, how do you spell 'sweater'?" A moment or two later, he asked, "How do you spell 'blouse'?" Being a little confused, I walked over to the table and looked over his shoulder. What I saw brought tears to my eyes. Stephen had carefully written out all the names of the people in his family... and next to them he was filling in what he would buy them for Christmas. The first thing he thought of when I said to make your Christmas list, was what he would buy to give to others. Even at the age of four, Stephen knew what God already knew... it is more blessed to give than to receive.

-Linda Lawson, Webb City, MO

Mains

Simple Christmas Turkey

Jennie Gist
Gooseberry Patch

This is by far the easiest way to make Christmas dinner. And just discard the oven bag after for super-easy clean-up!

salt and pepper to taste
12-lb. turkey, thawed if frozen
2 T. all-purpose flour

5 stalks celery, coarsely chopped
2 onions, quartered

Sprinkle salt and pepper over turkey to taste. Sprinkle the bottom of a turkey-size oven roasting bag with flour. Place celery and onions in bag; top with turkey. Seal bag with tie provided; poke several holes in the bag with a fork. Place in a roasting pan. Bake at 350 degrees for 3 to 3-1/2 hours, until a meat thermometer inserted in the thickest part of the thigh reaches 165 degrees. Let turkey rest for about 15 minutes before slicing. Serves 12.

My four children and I bake various kinds of cookies for several days during the month of December. We arrange them on platters for our family celebration after Midnight Mass. We also deliver them to friends and neighbors as Christmas Eve gifts and serve them to guests throughout the season. Our favorite baking day is the day we make sugar cookies, which is usually the weekend before Christmas Day. I roll, cut and bake while the kids sit at the long dining room table and decorate with icing, sprinkles and food coloring. All of my children are grown now, but the number of people around our table on Sugar Cookie Day is still growing, as they each bring spouses and a few more friends along for the day. We have so much fun and none of us wants to miss the day! Around Thanksgiving, everyone starts asking, "What's the date for Sugar Cookie Day?"

-Rosemary Cerny, Fairfax, VA

Turkey Meatloaf with Cranberry Glaze

Penny Sherman
Cumming, GA

*I like to change things up each year for Christmas dinner.
I made this recipe last year and discovered it's such a yummy
alternative to traditional holiday fare!*

16-oz. can jellied cranberry
    sauce, divided
1/2 c. chili sauce or catsup
1-1/4 lbs. lean ground turkey
1/2 lb. ground pork
1 egg, beaten

1 c. soft bread crumbs
1 onion, finely chopped
3/4 t. poultry seasoning
1/2 t. salt
1/8 t. pepper

Mix together 1/3 cup cranberry sauce and chili sauce or catsup.
In a bowl, combine turkey and remaining ingredients. Add 1/3 of
cranberry sauce mixture. Mix until well blended. Spoon into an
8"x4" loaf pan that has been sprayed lightly with non-stick vegetable
spray. Bake, uncovered, at 350 degrees for one hour. Top with
remaining cranberry sauce mixture and bake an additional 10 minutes.
Let stand for 10 minutes before slicing. Serve with remaining
cranberry sauce. Serves 6.

Set empty pie plates in a wire pie rack, then add two or three
tealights to each plate. Surround the tealights with bright
cranberries, tiny hemlock cones, sumac berries, cinnamon sticks,
star anise and whole cloves...a simple and natural centerpiece.

Apples & Chicken

Penny-Beth Faulkner
Westbrook, ME

A true taste of New England! Elegant and impressive
for Christmas dinner, informal or formal.

2 onions, chopped
5 T. butter
3 apples, peeled, cored and
   sliced
2 lbs. boneless, skinless chicken
   breasts
1 t. salt

1/2 t. pepper
1-1/4 c. shredded sharp
   Cheddar or Swiss cheese
1/2 c. grated Parmesan cheese
1/2 c. dry bread crumbs
2 T. applejack or apple cider

Being careful not to brown, sauté onions in butter in a skillet over medium heat until translucent. Line the bottom of a greased 13"x9" baking pan with apple slices. Arrange chicken over apples; sprinkle with salt and pepper. Top with onion mixture. Combine cheeses with bread crumbs and sprinkle on top. Drizzle with applejack or cider. Bake, covered, at 350 degrees for 30 minutes. Uncover and bake an additional 5 minutes, or until golden on top and chicken juices run clear. Serves 4.

A quick & easy side dish...quarter new potatoes and toss with a little olive oil, salt and pepper. Spread on a baking sheet and bake at 400 degrees until crisp and golden, 35 to 40 minutes.

Mains

Skillet Chicken Cordon Bleu

Barbara Horton
Cincinnati, OH

This easy dish is a favorite of my oldest son, Rick. I've shared this recipe with his wife who loves it too!

2 T. margarine
4 to 6 boneless, skinless
    chicken breasts
salt and pepper to taste
.87-oz. pkg. chicken gravy mix

3/4 c. water
1/4 c. dry white wine or
    apple juice
1/4 c. deli ham, chopped
1/4 c. shredded Swiss cheese

In a skillet over medium heat, melt margarine. Season chicken with salt and pepper and cook for 5 minutes or until browned; drain. In a bowl, combine gravy mix, water, wine or juice and ham. Pour gravy mixture over chicken in skillet. Reduce heat and simmer, partially covered, for 15 to 20 minutes, until chicken is cooked through. Remove chicken to a broiler pan; sprinkle with cheese and broil until cheese is melted. Serve chicken with gravy mixture. Serves 4 to 6.

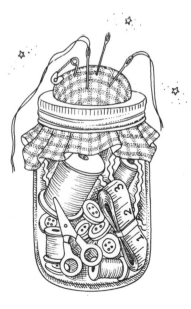

Create a sweet mini sewing kit..a handy gift! You'll need a pint-size Mason jar with a two-part lid. Pad the flat lid piece with cotton batting, cover with a circle of fabric and slide on the jar ring. Fill the jar with needles & thread, tiny scissors and a few spare buttons, screw on the lid and it's ready to use!

Lemon-Garlic Chicken

Kary Ross
Searcy, AR

*I bring this dish to families on the occasion of the birth of a baby.
It's that quick & easy to prepare! You can substitute one pound of
chicken tenders for chicken breasts, if desired.*

4 boneless, skinless chicken
   breasts
1/2 c. all-purpose flour
1/4 c. olive oil
2 T. garlic, minced

1 c. white wine or white
   grape juice
2 T. lemon juice
1/4 to 1/2 t. pepper

Coat chicken with flour; set aside. Heat olive oil in a large skillet over
medium heat; add garlic and chicken. Cook 8 minutes, turning once,
or until chicken is cooked through. Remove chicken from skillet and
keep warm. Add wine or grape juice, lemon juice and pepper to skillet,
stirring to loosen browned bits from bottom of skillet. Bring to a boil;
cook 10 minutes, or until juice mixture is reduced to about 1/2 cup.
Pour over chicken; serve immediately. Serves 4 to 6.

Are the kids getting cabin fever on a snowy day?
Send 'em outdoors with bottles of colored water to
squirt holiday messages on the freshly fallen snow.

Mains

Chicken & Rosemary Pizza

Teresa Podracky
Solon, OH

*In the summer, I use chicken that's been marinated in
Italian dressing and then grilled...delicious!*

2 c. shredded mozzarella cheese,
   divided
2 c. cooked chicken, chopped
1 c. red onion, sliced
1/4 c. fresh parsley, chopped
2 T. olive oil

2 cloves garlic, minced
1 T. fresh rosemary, chopped
1/2 t. salt
1/4 t. pepper
13.8-oz. tube refrigerated pizza
   dough

In a bowl, toss together 1-1/2 cups cheese and remaining ingredients
except pizza dough. Roll out dough onto a lightly greased baking
sheet. Spread cheese mixture onto dough to within 1/2 inch of the
edge. Sprinkle with remaining cheese. Bake at 425 degrees for 18 to
22 minutes, until golden. Let stand 10 minutes before slicing and
serving. Serves 4 to 6.

Display holiday cards throughout the house so they'll be
enjoyed in every room. Tape a variety of patterned and
solid ribbons to doors...vertically, horizontally or in a grid.
Use double-stick tape to attach cards to the ribbons.

Quick & Easy Creamy Chicken

Eri Niska
Fort Wayne, IN

I have been making this chicken since I was in college, a long time ago. The chicken is moist and yummy. To cook in a slow cooker, brown the chicken first, add all the ingredients except rice and cook on the low setting for eight hours.

4 boneless, skinless chicken
   breasts, cut into bite-size
   pieces
salt and pepper to taste
2 T. butter

1 onion, sliced
Optional: 8-oz. pkg. sliced
   mushrooms
1 c. whipping cream
cooked rice

Season chicken with salt and pepper; set aside. Melt butter in a large skillet over medium-high heat; add onion and mushrooms, if using, and sauté until tender. Add chicken and brown on both sides. Reduce heat to low and stir in cream. Simmer until chicken is cooked through and tender, about 20 minutes. Serve over rice. Serves 4 to 6.

Wrap up some fragrant potpourri in dainty embroidered handkerchiefs and tie with gingham ribbon. Place in a bowl to use as little gifts for visitors.

Mains

Trim-the-Tree Casserole

Vickie

*A six-ingredient favorite! Pop it in the oven while you
string the lights on the Christmas tree and hang the stockings.*

4 boneless, skinless chicken
    breasts, pounded 1/2-inch
    thick
4 slices Swiss cheese
10-3/4 oz. can cream of broccoli
    soup

1/3 c. milk
1 c. herb-flavored stuffing mix,
    crushed
1/4 c. butter, melted

Place chicken breasts in a greased 13"x9" baking pan. Top with
cheese. Stir together soup and milk. Spread over cheese. Toss stuffing
mix with melted butter and sprinkle over all. Bake, uncovered, at
350 degrees for 30 minutes, or until chicken is tender and cooked
through. Serves 4 to 6.

Illuminate your tree with the perfect amount of lights.
An eight-foot tree shimmers and glows with 125 to
150 large bulbs or 400 small ones.

Cheesy Chicken & Biscuits

Darcy Geiger
Columbia City, IN

I was just playing around with these ingredients one afternoon and created this easy dish...my husband and three young children loved it!

32-oz. pkg. pasteurized process
   cheese spread, cubed
10-3/4 oz. can cream of chicken
   soup
1/2 c. sour cream

1 c. milk
4 to 6 cooked chicken breasts,
   cubed
8 to 10 warm biscuits, cut into
   bite-size pieces

In a saucepan over low heat, stir together cheese, soup, sour cream and milk; heat through. Add chicken; cook an additional 10 minutes over low heat, stirring occasionally. Serve over warm biscuits. Serves 4 to 6.

A warm fruit compote is a delightful change from tossed salads.
Simmer frozen cut-up peaches, blueberries and raspberries
together with a little honey, lemon juice and cinnamon,
just until syrupy and tender.

Mains

Chicken & Dressing Bake

Dueley Lucas
Somerset, KY

A great dish for family, company or church gatherings.

2 6-oz. pkgs. cornbread
   stuffing mix
1 t. dried sage
1/4 t. pepper
1 onion, finely chopped
4 stalks celery, finely chopped
2 10-3/4 oz. cans cream of
   chicken soup

2 c. chicken broth
2 c. shredded Cheddar cheese,
   divided
4 boneless, skinless chicken
   breasts, cooked and cut in
   half lengthwise

In a large bowl, mix together stuffing mix, sage and pepper. Add onion and celery. Add soup, broth and one cup cheese to stuffing mixture; mix well. Place stuffing mixture into a 13"x9" baking pan that has been sprayed with non-stick vegetable spray. Place chicken on top of stuffing mixture. Top with remaining cheese. Bake, covered, at 350 degrees for 30 minutes. Makes 8 servings.

Choose a theme for holiday decorating...Silver Bells,
Farmhouse Kitchen, A White Christmas are a few ideas.
Then carry out your theme throughout the house...Christmas
tree ornaments, the front door wreath, the garland on
the mantel and even a dinner table centerpiece. Clever!

Curried Chicken-Broccoli Casserole
Kathy Arner
Phoenix, AZ

My wonderful mother-in-law fixed this quick recipe all the time. Also terrific with turkey leftovers at the holidays. If you make this ahead of time, place the casserole in the oven as it preheats to gradually heat up. Serve with fresh rolls, fruit or salad.

10-3/4 oz. can cream of chicken
   soup
1 t. lemon juice
1/4 to 1/2 t. curry powder
1/2 c. mayonnaise
10-oz. pkg. frozen chopped
   broccoli, thawed and drained

2 c. chicken, cooked and
   chopped
1 c. shredded Cheddar cheese
1/4 c. dry bread crumbs

In a bowl, combine soup, lemon juice, curry powder and mayonnaise. Place broccoli in a greased 9"x9" baking pan. Add chicken. Pour soup mixture over chicken; stir to mix all. Top with Cheddar cheese and sprinkle bread crumbs on top. Bake, uncovered, at 350 degrees for 45 minutes, or until golden and bubbly. Serves 4 to 6.

Create a festive casserole topper. Unfold two refrigerated
pie crusts; sprinkle one with pecans and sun-dried tomatoes
(or any other goodies) and top with remaining crust. Roll
crusts together and cut into shapes with cookie cutters.
Bake at 425 degrees for 8 minutes and arrange on
the casserole before serving.

Tina's Easy Chicken & Dumplings

Tina Goodpasture
Meadowview, VA

I just love chicken & dumplings during the winter.
My Grandmother Hudson always made dumplings from scratch.
I cheat a little and use canned biscuits!

32-oz. container chicken broth
3 c. chicken, cooked and
  shredded
10-3/4 oz. can cream of chicken
  soup

1/4 t. poultry seasoning
10-oz. tube refrigerated jumbo
  buttermilk biscuits
2 carrots, peeled and sliced
3 stalks celery, diced

In a Dutch oven over medium-high heat, mix together broth, chicken, soup and seasoning; bring to a boil. Cover, reduce heat to low and simmer, stirring occasionally. Meanwhile, place biscuits on a lightly floured surface. Roll or pat each biscuit to 1/8-inch thickness; cut into 1/2-inch wide strips. Drop strips one at a time into broth mixture. Add carrots and celery. Cover and simmer 15 to 30 minutes, until vegetables are tender and dumplings are done, stirring occasionally to prevent dumplings from sticking. Serves 4 to 6.

Not enough ribbon to tie a bow? Wrap a box in
solid paper, then hot-glue wrapped peppermint candies
to the box top...so cute!

Teriyaki Chicken

Amy Holt
Enterprise, UT

I have to triple this recipe when I make it for my family. I love it because it is quick & easy to put together. I have even put all the ingredients except the rice in my slow cooker and let it cook on the low setting all day.

2/3 c. soy sauce
1/3 c. sugar
1/4 t. ground ginger
1/8 t. garlic powder

4 to 5 boneless, skinless
chicken breasts
cooked rice

In a skillet over medium heat, whisk together soy sauce, sugar, ginger and garlic powder. When heated through, add chicken. Cover and simmer, basting chicken occasionally with sauce, for about 30 minutes, or until chicken is cooked through. Uncover and cook an additional 10 minutes, or until sauce thickens. Serve with rice. Serves 4 to 6.

Craft this heartfelt gift for a special friend. Cover buttons
with holiday fabric, then glue to ribbons; let glue dry.
Tie around napkins for the easiest napkin rings!

Mains

Mr. Dillon's Prime Rib

Terry Dillon
Parma, OH

My family owned a restaurant in Ashland, Ohio called Mr. Dillon's. Prime rib was a specialty I made every Wednesday, Friday and Saturday. Customers would make reservations for themselves and the prime rib. Most nights we sold out by eight-thirty! One year the American Legion I belonged to talked me into preparing it for the whole club. I had to use electric roasters set up all over the building. I made around twenty that night. Everyone was thrilled, but I told them if they wanted it again, they would have to come to the restaurant! I prefer this moist roast method even though most restaurants dry roast. Your butcher can remove the fat cap and tie it back on. I like cutting the bones off the roast in one whole piece and saving them for another day to broil with barbecue sauce.

16 to 18-lb. standing beef rib
   roast, cap removed and
   tied on
1 T. white pepper
1 c. beef-flavored soup base or
   3/4 c. beef bouillon granules

1 onion, quartered and
   separated into petals
1 t. browning and seasoning
   sauce

Place roast, cap-side up, in a large roasting pan with lid. Fill with 1/2 inch of water. Season roast with pepper and soup base or bouillon. Arrange onion around and on top of roast. Cover and bake at 325 degrees for 3-1/2 to 4 hours, until a meat thermometer inserted in the center reads 150 degrees for medium rare, 160 degrees for medium, or 170 degrees for well-done. The end pieces will be more well-done and roast will be rarer toward the middle. Transfer roast to a cutting board; let stand 10 to 15 minutes. Meanwhile, to make the au jus, pour pan drippings through a paper towel-lined strainer into a saucepan. Allow to stand for one minute; use a soup ladle to skim off fat. Add browning and seasoning sauce to pan; reheat. Remove strings and cap from roast; discard. Remove bones and carve into one to 1-1/2 inch slices. Arrange on a serving platter and pour au jus around meat. Makes about 14 servings.

Cheater's Beef Stroganoff

Donna Bizub
Perrysville, OH

My mother worked full-time and raised five children on her own. She was always looking for something she could whip up quickly. One Christmas she served stroganoff and we have been making it ever since. Good for a weekday meal and just as impressive for company...it always gets rave reviews!

1 lb. stew beef, cubed
10-3/4 oz. can golden
　　mushroom soup
10-3/4 oz. can French onion
　　soup

cooked noodles or mashed
　　potatoes

Combine beef and soups in a lightly greased 2-quart casserole dish. Bake, covered, at 350 degrees for 2 hours, stirring frequently. Serve over noodles or mashed potatoes. Serves 4 to 6.

Cook egg noodles the easy way...no watching needed.
Bring water to a rolling boil, then turn off heat. Add noodles
and let stand for 20 minutes, stirring twice.

Easy Beef Pot Pie

Sarah Stillman
Salt Lake City, UT

*My kids love when I put the pie crust in muffin tins
and serve individual pot pies!*

1 lb. lean ground beef, browned
  and drained
10-3/4 oz. can cream of potato
  soup
10-3/4 oz. can cream of
  mushroom soup

1/2 c. beef broth
2 c. frozen mixed vegetables
1 t. garlic powder
salt and pepper to taste
2 9-inch pie crusts

Mix together all ingredients except pie crusts. Line an ungreased
9" pie plate with one pie crust. Pour beef mixture into crust; top with
second crust. Seal edges; cut a slit in top of crust. Bake at 425 degrees
for 30 to 35 minutes, until golden. Makes 6 servings.

Is your mantel perfectly decorated this year? Take snapshots
of your favorite Christmas nooks and tuck them in with your
Christmas decorations. Next year when you unpack your storage
boxes, you'll know just how to arrange all those trinkets!

Big Eddie's Rigatoni

Mary Beth Laporte
Escanaba, MI

This recipe was created by my eighty-four-year-old father who has always been a great cook and is affectionately called "Big Eddie" by family members. A delicious and satisfying meal when paired with salad and garlic bread.

16-oz. pkg. rigatoni pasta, uncooked
1/8 t. salt
2 lbs. lean ground beef
1-1/2 oz. pkg. spaghetti sauce mix
45-oz. jar chunky tomato, garlic and onion pasta sauce

8 slices mozzarella cheese, divided
8 slices provolone cheese, divided
8-oz. container sour cream
Garnish: grated Parmesan cheese

Cook pasta according to package directions; drain, mix in salt and set aside. Meanwhile, in a large, deep skillet over medium heat, brown ground beef; drain. Stir in spaghetti sauce mix and pasta sauce; heat through. In a greased 13"x9" baking pan, layer half the pasta, 4 slices mozzarella cheese and 4 slices provolone cheese. Spread entire container of sour cream across top. Layer half of ground beef mixture. Repeat layering, except for sour cream, ending with ground beef mixture. Garnish with Parmesan cheese. Bake, uncovered, at 350 degrees for 30 minutes, or until bubbly. Serves 8.

A pat of homemade garlic butter really adds flavor to warm bread or steamed vegetables. Blend equal parts of softened butter and olive oil, then stir in finely chopped garlic to taste...so easy!

Mains

4-Generation Goulash

Debra Bailey
Cedar Lake, IN

My mom made this goulash while I was growing up. In the winter she ladled it over mashed potatoes. I've passed this recipe down to my daughter and granddaughter. So that makes four generations!

1-1/2 c. elbow macaroni,
  uncooked
2 lbs. lean ground beef
1 onion, chopped

2 15-oz. cans tomato sauce
1 to 2 14-1/2 oz. cans stewed
  tomatoes
15-oz. can corn, drained

Cook macaroni according to package directions; drain. Meanwhile, in a Dutch over medium heat, brown together ground beef and onion; drain. Add cooked macaroni and remaining ingredients; stir to mix. Reduce heat to medium-low and simmer until heated through, stirring occasionally. Serves 6 to 8.

It's fun to mix & match...set a festive table with items you already have! Green transferware serving bowls, sparkling white porcelain dinner plates and ruby-red stemmed glasses combine beautifully with Christmas dinnerware.

Beef & Rice Skillet

Crista Stonebraker
Columbus, OH

*I threw this together one night before we were married. It is still
my husband's response to "What do you want for supper?"*

2 T. butter
6.9-oz. pkg. beef-flavored rice
   vermicelli mix
3 c. beef broth

Optional: 8-oz. can sliced
   mushrooms, drained
1 lb. ground beef, browned and
   drained

In a large skillet over medium heat, melt butter. Add rice and cook
until golden, stirring occasionally. Carefully pour in broth, seasoning
packet from rice and mushrooms, if using. Add ground beef; reduce
heat and cover. Simmer for about 15 minutes. Serves 4.

I started this tradition as a way to help me wrap gifts easily
when my three children were very young. I pick a certain pattern
of gift wrap for each child and don't put any names on the gifts.
On Christmas Eve, they guess who each stack belongs to and
if they're right, they get to pick when to open the presents.
They're in their thirties now and we still do this. With five
grandchildren it gets a little difficult...I have to write a note
to myself because it's too hard to remember!

-Marcie Shaffer, Taneytown, MD

Fric-A-Dilli

Sharyn Mowrey
Carey, OH

This recipe came from one of my aunts. It's so versatile!
I have changed it by using chicken, mixing in peas or sprinkling
French fried onions or coarsely ground pepper on top.

1 lb. ground beef, browned and
    drained
salt and pepper to taste
1/4 to 1/2 c. onion, diced
2 to 3 slices bread, toasted and
    diced

10-3/4 oz. can cream of chicken
    or cream of mushroom soup
2/3 c. water

Place ground beef in a lightly greased 9"x9" baking pan. Season with salt and pepper. Mix in onion and bread. In a bowl, combine soup and water; pour over all. Mix lightly. Bake, uncovered, at 375 degrees for 30 to 35 minutes, until bubbly. Serves 4 to 6.

To make a snowman bag, fold down the top of a white lunch sack; round the edges with scissors. Add eyes and a mouth using a black pen. Glue on an orange craft foam nose. Top him off with an infant-size hat!

Marry-Me-Matt Enchiladas

Kim Bryan
Whitehouse, TX

*This is the recipe that got my husband to marry me! I made this
for him when we were dating...we were married within a year!
If you're looking to get hitched, try this dish!*

1-1/2 lbs. lean ground beef
1/2 onion, chopped
2 T. enchilada sauce mix
10-oz. can mild enchilada sauce
10-3/4 oz. can cream of
   mushroom soup

10 to 12 flour tortillas
2 c. shredded Colby Jack cheese,
   divided

In a large skillet over medium heat, brown ground beef and onion;
drain. Stir in dry enchilada sauce mix. In a small saucepan over
medium-low heat, combine enchilada sauce and soup; heat through,
stirring occasionally. Remove from heat and dip tortillas into sauce
mixture to keep them moist. Divide ground beef mixture evenly over
tortillas. Sprinkle one cup cheese evenly across tortillas. Roll up; place
in a lightly greased 13"x9" baking pan. Pour remaining enchilada
sauce mixture over all; sprinkle with remaining cheese. Cover with
aluminum foil. Bake at 350 degrees for about 30 minutes, or until
cheese is bubbly. Serves 5 to 6.

Enchilada casserole! Instead of rolling up tortillas
enchilada style, just cut into strips, layer filling and sauce
and bake until heated through.

Mains

Taco Pasta Skillet

Jackie Flood
Geneseo, NY

*My husband and I are very fond of Mexican dishes and this is
one of our favorites. I took a couple different recipes and tweaked
each to come up with this one-pan meal. So filling and rich!*

1/2 lb. lean ground beef,
   browned and drained
1-1/4 oz. pkg. taco seasoning
   mix
11-oz. can corn, drained
14-oz. can black beans, drained
   and rinsed

1 c. salsa
3 c. hot water
1 c. penne pasta, uncooked
1/2 c. cream cheese, softened
1 c. shredded Mexican-blend
   cheese

Place all ingredients except cheeses in a large, deep skillet over
medium heat; mix well. Simmer for 15 minutes, or until pasta is
tender. Stir in cheeses and continue to cook until cheese is melted.
Serves 6.

A real conversation starter...ask older relatives about their
earliest holiday memories. Did they have a Christmas tree?
How was it decorated? Do they recall setting out cookies &
milk for Santa? Don't miss the opportunity to preserve
these sweet memories on video.

Orange-Glazed Pork Chops

Barb Rudyk
Alberta, Canada

Mmm...serve with buttery noodles and steamed green veggies.

1 T. oil
4 pork chops, 3/4-inch thick
1/2 c. orange juice

2 T. brown sugar, packed
2 T. orange marmalade
1 T. vinegar

Heat oil in a large skillet over medium heat; brown pork chops on both sides. Drain and transfer to a lightly greased 11"x7" baking pan. Combine remaining ingredients and pour over pork chops. Bake, uncovered, at 350 degrees for 35 for 40 minutes, until pork chops are tender. Serves 4.

A garland of walnuts is a rustic decoration that will keep for many years. Drill through whole, unshelled walnuts with a 7/64 or smaller drill bit. String with wire and tie on ribbon. Store your garland with mothballs or cedar chips to keep unwanted pests away.

Mains

Ham & Potato Casserole

Linda Ervin
Durant, OK

I first made this casserole when there was ham left over from Christmas. Now my family requests it each year...and every time we have leftover ham!

4 potatoes, peeled and cubed
1 lb. cooked ham, cubed
1/2 c. onion, chopped
10-3/4 oz. can cream of
   mushroom or cream of
   chicken soup

1-1/4 c. milk
1-1/2 c. favorite shredded
   cheese, divided
salt and pepper to taste

Place potatoes in a saucepan filled with boiling salted water; cook over medium-high heat until almost tender, about 12 to 15 minutes. Drain and place in the bottom of a lightly greased 13"x9" baking pan. Sprinkle ham and onion on top of potatoes. Mix together soup, milk and one cup cheese; pour over top of potato mixture. Sprinkle with remaining cheese. Bake, uncovered, at 350 degrees for 25 minutes, or until hot and bubbly. At serving time, season with salt and pepper to taste. Serves 4.

Turn a toboggan into a clever wintertime serving table!
Just set it securely on top of a buffet table, toss on a plaid throw,
and then load it up with lots of salads, sides and breads.

Saucy Pork Chops

Sharon Crider
Junction City, KS

A deliciously speedy way to serve pork chops. So good!

1 T. oil
4 pork chops, 1/2-inch thick
1/4 c. water

10-3/4 oz. can cream of onion
soup

Heat oil in a skillet over medium heat; brown pork chops on both sides, about 8 minutes. Drain and set aside. Add water and soup to skillet, stirring together, and bring to a boil. Return pork chops to skillet. Reduce heat to low. Cover and cook 5 minutes, or until pork chops are cooked through. Serves 4.

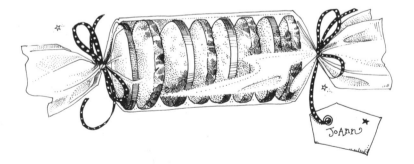

Hosting a holiday dinner party? Stack a few cookies at each place setting and tie up with bright ribbon...a sweet surprise for each guest.

Sweet-and-Sour Pork
& Sauerkraut

Doris Butler
Vero Beach, FL

*I came up with this dish on my own. I make it every New Year's Day
for good luck. My friends & family love it! This recipe makes a large
amount...enough to share with a group or freeze for later.*

4 14-1/2 oz. pkgs. sauerkraut,
   divided
16-oz. pkg. dark brown sugar

5 to 7-lb. boneless pork butt
   roast, cut into 6 pieces
hot mashed potatoes

In a large roasting pan with lid, empty 2 packages of sauerkraut with
liquid. Sprinkle with brown sugar. Drain remaining sauerkraut and
add to pan; mix well. Arrange pork evenly into sauerkraut mixture.
Cover and bake at 325 degrees for about 2 hours, or until pork shreds
easily. Remove pork from pan and shred with 2 forks; return to pan.
Increase oven to 350 degrees. Bake, uncovered, stirring occasionally,
for an additional hour, or until golden and most liquid has cooked off.
Serve over mashed potatoes. Makes 16 servings.

For a touch of old-fashioned cheer, use vintage
alphabet blocks to spell out holiday greetings
on a mantel or buffet.

Southern Sausage & Pintos

Tammy Rogers
Gordonsville, VA

*This recipe is quick to prepare, simple to double for a larger crowd
and delicious served with hot cornbread.*

1 lb. pork sausage links
1 onion, chopped
1 green pepper, chopped

2 15-oz. cans pinto beans,
   drained
8-oz. can tomato sauce

Cook sausages until browned on all sides in a large skillet over
medium heat; drain all but 2 tablespoons drippings. Cut each sausage
into thirds; return to skillet. Add onion and green pepper; sauté until
tender. Add remaining ingredients. Stir and simmer for 10 minutes,
until heated through. Serves 6.

Turn your Christmas tree into a scrapbook. Photocopy favorite
family pictures, glue them to silver paper then adhere
rick rack to the edges for homespun frames.

Mains

Cheesy Sausage, Noodle & Broccoli Bake

Jennifer Devening
Freetown, IN

Cheesy and delicious...be ready to dish up seconds!

2 c. rotini pasta, uncooked
16-oz. pkg. smoked pork
   sausage, cut into 1/4-inch
   to 1/2-inch slices

16-oz. pkg. frozen broccoli,
   thawed
15-oz. jar pasteurized process
   cheese sauce

Cook pasta according to package directions; drain. Combine pasta and remaining ingredients; place in a lightly greased 2-quart casserole dish. Bake, uncovered, at 375 degrees for 30 minutes. Serves 6.

Carrying in a casserole? Be sure to tie on a tag with the recipe! Clever tags can be made from holiday cards or colorful scrapbooking paper.

Cheesy Rice & Ham

Robin Arnold
Fort Worth, TX

My mother made this comforting casserole when I was a child. Now my teenage son will request it for his birthday dinner! A perfect way to use up leftover ham and easily halved for a smaller casserole.

2 c. milk
2 c. shredded Cheddar cheese
2 c. cooked rice
4 eggs, beaten

1/4 t. salt
1/8 t. pepper
2 c. cooked ham, diced
paprika to taste

In a medium saucepan, bring milk to a boil over medium-low heat. Turn off heat and mix in cheese, rice, eggs, salt and pepper. Blend until smooth and add ham. Spoon into a greased 13"x9" baking pan. Sprinkle with paprika. Bake, uncovered, at 350 degrees for 35 minutes, or until golden on top. Serves 6.

A special treat for your holiday guests...leave personalized, beribboned ornaments on their pillows in the guest room.

Mains

Pineapple-Clove Ham Glaze

Teresa Stiegelmeyer
Indianapolis, IN

Pour this glaze over your holiday ham and baste every fifteen minutes. It tastes as good as the expensive spiral hams at specialty stores. You can also garnish with cherries and whole cloves inside each pineapple slice. Showy!

1 c. brown sugar, packed
1 t. dry mustard
1 t. ground cloves

1 T. all-purpose flour
20-oz. can sliced pineapple,
    drained and juice reserved

Mix brown sugar, spices and flour together. Moisten mixture to a thin paste consistency with reserved pineapple juice. Reserve pineapple slices to garnish ham, if desired. Makes about one cup.

Raisin Sauce for Baked Ham

Sharon Matheisen
Scio, OR

This is a recipe that was passed down to me by my mother-in-law Irene. If I had to guess, I would say it's well over eighty years old. It was always a favorite with the men in our family. Everything she cooked for us all she made with love.

12 whole cloves
3/4 c. raisins
1 c. cold water
3/4 c. sugar
2 T. all-purpose flour

1/16 t. pepper
1 T. vinegar
2 T. orange juice
1 T. butter
1 T. lemon juice

Tie cloves in a piece of cheesecloth. In a saucepan over medium heat, cook cloves, raisins and water until raisins are tender. In a bowl, mix sugar, flour and pepper. Add to raisin mixture. Cook until thickened. Stir in remaining ingredients. Heat through and remove cloves. Makes about 2-1/2 cups.

Nonna Mina's Christmas Eve Sauce *Ashley Billings*
Norfolk, VA

My Nonna Mina made this fish sauce every year on Christmas Eve because, as Catholics, we were not supposed to eat meat on this day. However, when we were younger, my sister Chantel and I hated fish, even though we'd never actually tried it! So, Nonna obliged us and always made a separate meat sauce for our spaghetti. Now that I've "matured" into liking fish, I make this sauce for my husband and me on Christmas Eve, along with a fish platter consisting of shrimp, scallops, king crab legs and lobster.

2 to 3 cloves garlic, chopped	1/8 t. pepper
1 T. olive oil	1/8 t. Italian seasoning
2 29-oz. cans tomato sauce	1/8 t. dried oregano
1 lb. cooked medium shrimp	1/8 t. dried basil
1/8 t. salt	cooked spaghetti

Cook garlic in olive oil in a saucepan over medium heat for 5 to 6 minutes, until just starting to turn golden. Remove and discard garlic, leaving oil in pan. Add remaining ingredients except spaghetti. Cook for 30 minutes, stirring occasionally. Serve over spaghetti. Serves 6 to 8.

Have a Christmas Eve buffet without the fuss.
Split the meal into courses and let guests choose a course
to bring...spend less time in the kitchen and more
with family & friends!

Mains

Honey-Mustard Glazed Salmon

Chris Yuva
Dublin, OH

*A quick-to-fix dish packed with flavor and
easily doubled or tripled.*

1 T. light brown sugar, packed
1 T. butter, melted
1 T. olive oil
1 T. honey

1 T. soy sauce
1 T. Dijon mustard
1 clove garlic, chopped
2 7-oz. salmon fillets

In a small bowl, mix all ingredients except salmon. Place salmon in a
shallow glass dish. Pour marinade over salmon. Cover and refrigerate
15 minutes to one hour, turning salmon often. Transfer salmon to a
lightly greased 9"x9" baking pan. Broil 10 to 12 minutes, or until
salmon flakes easily with a fork, brushing one to 3 times with
marinade. Discard remaining marinade. Serves 2.

Wrapped in love! Use children's drawings as wrapping
paper for gifts from the kitchen. Perfect for
grandparents and aunts & uncles.

Crabmeat Casserole

Beckie Butcher
Elgin, IL

*My mother made this for us every winter, and it truly lives up to the
term, "comfort food." There's nothing like a yummy, rich casserole to
stick to your ribs during winter in Chicago.*

1 c. milk
8-oz. pkg. pasteurized process
   cheese spread, cubed
1/2 c. butter, softened
4-oz. jar chopped pimentos,
   drained

1-1/2 c. egg noodles, cooked
1 to 2 6-oz. cans lump
   crabmeat, drained
1/4 c. dry bread crumbs

In a bowl, combine all ingredients except bread crumbs. Transfer to a
greased 2-quart casserole dish. Sprinkle with bread crumbs. Bake,
uncovered, at 350 degrees for 30 minutes. Serves 4.

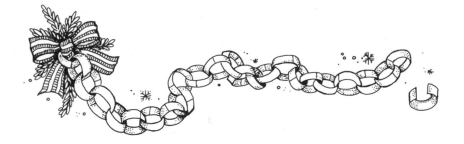

Make a happiness chain to wind around the tree. Cut strips of
colorful paper and have family members write a few words
on each strip about what makes them feel happy..."my cat
Fluffy," "making snow angels" and so on. Tape strips together
into loops to form a chain...sure to bring smiles!

Mains

Speedy Tuna & Noodles

Jamie Johnson
Gooseberry Patch

I really had a craving to eat tuna noodle casserole one night but I didn't have the ingredients to make it. So I went into my kitchen to see what I had. I liked what I made so much I had it the next night too! If you only have regular Alfredo sauce, you can add a teaspoon or two of garlic powder.

1 c. cooked linguine pasta
1/8 t. salt
2 6-oz. cans tuna, drained

15-oz. jar roasted garlic Alfredo
sauce

Place pasta, salt and tuna into a saucepan over medium heat. Add desired amount of sauce. Stir to combine; cook just until heated through, about 5 minutes. Serves one to 2.

When heading out for wintertime fun, bring extras...spare mittens, socks, sweaters and hats to replace wet ones. And don't forget a thermos of chocolatey cocoa and extra blankets for keeping warm & cozy.

A's Mushroom Pie

Elizabeth VanDeursen
Homewood, IL

My four sisters and I got together every Christmas with our mother to create a new Christmas memory. This was one of the many dishes we all shared and loved.

2 10-3/4 oz. cans cream of
   mushroom soup
6 4-oz. cans sliced mushrooms,
   drained
3 T. beef or chicken bouillon
   granules

9-inch pie crust, baked
1/3 c. shredded mozzarella
   cheese
1/3 c. shredded sharp Cheddar
   cheese

Set aside half of one can of soup for another use. Mix together remaining 1-1/2 cans soup, mushrooms and bouillon in a bowl. Pour into pie crust and sprinkle cheeses evenly over top. Cover edges of crust with aluminum foil. Bake, uncovered, at 350 degrees for about 30 minutes, or until cheese is bubbly and golden. Makes 6 to 8 servings.

An afternoon of cutting and decorating a fresh pine tree can leave sticky fingers of sap! For a quick clean-up, pour a tablespoon of olive oil onto a cloth, then rub until clean...also works as a moisturizer for dry winter skin.

Mains

Hearty Mushroom Skillet

Shelley Turner
Boise, ID

Our New Year's Day tradition is to serve breakfast for dinner!
We like this colorful, tasty dish served with hot, buttered
biscuits and warm maple syrup.

2 lbs. redskin potatoes, cubed
2 T. olive oil
1 green pepper, sliced
1 red pepper, sliced
1 onion, sliced

2 c. sliced mushrooms
salt and pepper to taste
3 c. shredded sharp Cheddar
   cheese
6 eggs, beaten

Add potatoes to a stockpot filled with water; bring to a boil. Cook until tender but still firm, 12 to 15 minutes; drain. Heat olive oil in a large, deep skillet over medium heat; add potatoes and cook until golden on all sides. Add remaining ingredients except cheese and eggs. Cook until vegetables are tender; add cheese, stirring to melt. In a separate skillet, scramble eggs as desired. To serve, top potato mixture with eggs. Serves 6.

Make it easy on yourself when planning holiday dinners...stick to tried & true recipes! You'll find your guests are just as happy with simple comfort foods as with the most elegant gourmet meal.

Fast-Fix Penne Alfredo

Tiffany Brinkley
Broomfield, CO

So rich and cheesy...a real comfort food for a chilly evening!

16-oz. pkg. penne pasta,
   uncooked
1 c. whipping cream
1/2 c. butter, softened
1/2 c. grated Parmesan cheese

1/2 c. fresh parsley, chopped
1 t. salt
1/4 t. pepper
1/8 t. garlic powder

Bring a large pot of lightly salted water to a boil. Add pasta and cook for 8 to 10 minutes, until al dente; drain. Combine cream and butter in a Dutch oven over medium-low heat. Heat until butter melts, stirring occasionally; be careful not to bring mixture to a boil. Stir in remaining ingredients. Toss with cooked pasta and serve immediately. Makes 8 servings.

Every year, Grandma, my aunts and pretty much all the women of my Italian side of the family would spend what seemed like months baking, cooking and preparing for Christmas. Christmas Eve would find my Great-Grandmother's house full of family who all brought their appetites. We ate fresh, homemade pasta and all the goodies the women-folk had spent so much time and love preparing. My dad loved every morsel. When I was about four years old, he ate so much that he told my mom, "I'm so full, I don't think I can eat for four days"...and he didn't! Those were the good old days!

-Pam Schlimmer, San Jose, CA

Mains

Spicy Baked Linguine

Patty Flak
Erie, PA

*Easy to assemble and bake at a later time...perfect for family members
with newborn babies. They get a home-cooked meal without
having to do a lot of work. Just bake and it's time to eat!*

16-oz. pkg. linguine pasta,
   uncooked
1 T. oil
1 zucchini, cut into one-inch
   chunks
1 red pepper, cut into one-inch
   chunks

26-oz. jar spaghetti sauce
1 c. salsa
3/4 c. shredded mozzarella
   cheese

Cook pasta according to package directions; drain. Meanwhile, heat oil
in a stockpot over medium-high heat. Add zucchini and pepper; sauté
6 to 8 minutes. Stir in spaghetti sauce and salsa. Add pasta; mix well.
Place mixture in a 13"x9" baking pan that has been sprayed with
non-stick vegetable spray. Sprinkle with cheese. Bake, uncovered, at
350 degrees for 25 to 30 minutes. Serves 6 to 8.

Remember the birds at Christmastime. Decorate an outdoor
tree with suet balls, birdseed bells, garlands of fruit and
hollowed-out orange halves filled with birdseed.

Cabbage & Noodles

Debbie Muer
Encino, CA

*This Hungarian dish is so delicious, you can eat it
right out of the pot!*

16-oz. pkg. wide egg noodles,
   uncooked
1 head cabbage, shredded
1 to 2 onions, diced

1/4 c. oil
paprika to taste
salt and pepper to taste

Cook noodles according to package directions; drain. Meanwhile, in a
skillet over medium heat, sauté cabbage and onion in oil until golden,
about 20 to 30 minutes. Sprinkle paprika over cabbage mixture; stir in
noodles. Season with salt and pepper. Serves 8 to 10.

Some cards are just too pretty to toss after the holidays.
Trim them with decorative-edge scissors and quick as
a wink, they become gift tags, ornaments or placecards.

Desserts

Holiday Cranberry Trifle

Sonya Labbe
Los Angeles, CA

*This dessert is so beautiful. I love to entertain
with it...a perfect centerpiece for the holiday season.
Delicious with either fresh or frozen cranberries.*

2 12-oz. pkgs. cranberries
2-1/4 c. sugar, divided
zest of 1 orange
2 c. water
8-oz. pkg. cream cheese,
    softened

1/4 c. light brown sugar, packed
1/2 t. vanilla extract
2 c. whipping cream
2 all-butter pound cakes, cut
    into 3/4-inch thick slices

In a medium saucepan, combine cranberries, 2 cups sugar, zest and
water. Bring to a simmer over medium heat; cook until cranberries
begin to burst, about 8 to 10 minutes. Remove from heat; let cool
completely. Using an electric mixer on high speed, beat cream cheese,
brown sugar, remaining sugar and vanilla until well combined. With
electric mixer on medium speed, gradually add cream; continue
beating until soft peaks form. Arrange 1/3 of cake slices in a 3-quart
clear glass serving dish. Spoon 1/3 of cranberry mixture over cake;
spread to sides of dish. Dollop 1/3 of cream cheese mixture over
cranberry mixture; spread to sides of dish. Repeat twice, ending with
cream cheese mixture. Cover and refrigerate at least 2 hours before
serving. Serves 12.

Recycle holiday cards with
this sweet idea. Trace a
cookie-cutter shape around
the main image of the card.
Cut out the shape, punch a hole
and tie to a pine garland with
bright red ribbon or yarn.

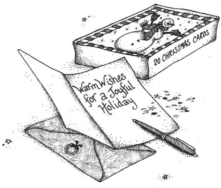

Desserts

Sycamore Farm Christmas Drink

Penny Arnold
Louisville, IL

The holidays are near when I begin making this drink at our family home in the country, appropriately named Sycamore Farm.

64-oz. bottle cranberry juice
64-oz. bottle apple juice
1/2 c. orange juice
1 T. cinnamon

1 T. whole cloves
2/3 c. sugar
Garnish: orange slices and
   cinnamon sticks

Combine all ingredients except garnish in a large stockpot over medium heat. Stir often until heated through. Remove cloves. Garnish with orange slices and cinnamon sticks. Makes 16 cups.

Baked Brandied Cranberries

Ellen Den Boer-Hacquebard
Midwolde, Netherlands

I am Dutch and the only way we prepare cranberries is by cooking them in sugary water. One of my American friends gave me this recipe she received some twenty-five years ago from her neighbor.

2 12-oz. pkgs. cranberries
2-1/3 c. sugar, divided

1/4 c. brandy or apple juice

Place cranberries in an ungreased glass 13"x9" baking pan. Top with 2 cups of sugar; do not stir. Cover tightly with aluminum foil. Bake at 350 degrees for 50 to 55 minutes, until cranberries burst. Remove foil and stir. Let stand 10 minutes. Drizzle with brandy or apple juice. Stir in remaining sugar. Cool to room temperature; cover and refrigerate. Serves 6 to 8.

Cherry Christmas Pizza

Jacquelynn Daunce
Lockport, NY

I try to make our Christmas a little less stressful with very simple, great-tasting recipes! I can put this recipe together in less than ten minutes. While it's baking and cooling, I can wrap a handful of gifts, set the dinner table and join in a chorus of "Jingle Bells"! Any kind of canned pie filling may be used...apple, blueberry, peach...but cherry looks so festive for the holidays.

9-inch frozen pie crust, thawed
8-oz. pkg. cream cheese,
   softened
2 eggs, beaten

1/2 c. sugar
1 t. vanilla extract
21-oz. can cherry pie filling

Lay thawed pie crust flat onto a 12" pizza pan that has been sprayed with non-stick vegetable spray. Pat crust to sides of pan. Bake at 425 degrees for 15 minutes. Let cool; reduce oven temperature to 375 degrees. Beat cream cheese, eggs, sugar and vanilla in a medium bowl. Pour over crust. Bake at 375 degrees for 15 minutes. Let cool; spread pie filling over top. Serves 8.

Dress up a mailbox using holiday stencils, fabric, greenery and bows. Fill with fun little treasures collected throughout the year. Place it on the table in the front hall and have young guests check to see if they've received mail!

Desserts

Fast & Easy Cherry Cheesecake

Angela Rowe
Ontario, Canada

My mom and I make this simple no-bake dessert
every year for Christmas. Enjoy!

8-oz. pkg. cream cheese,
   softened
1 c. sugar
1/2 c. cold milk

1 env. whipped topping mix
1/2 t. vanilla extract
2 9-inch graham cracker crusts
21-oz. can cherry pie filing

Blend together cream cheese and sugar with an electric mixer on medium speed until smooth, about 2 to 3 minutes. In a separate bowl, combine cold milk, whipped topping mix and vanilla. Beat with an electric mixer on high speed for 4 minutes. Lightly fold milk mixture into cream cheese mixture. Pour mixture into crusts; spread pie filling evenly across both cheesecakes. Cover and refrigerate overnight. Makes 2 cheesecakes, 6 servings each.

If you've strung your Christmas tree with popcorn,
be sure to hang the garlands outside for the birds
after the tree comes down!

Shelle's Millionaire Pie

Michelle Caldwell
Totz, KY

I have been making this no-bake pie for Christmas since I was in high school and it has become a tradition. The recipe makes three pies...one for the parents, one for the in-laws and one for home.

2 8-oz. containers frozen
   whipped topping, thawed
14-oz. can sweetened
   condensed milk
20-oz. can crushed pineapple,
   drained

1 c. chopped walnuts
1/4 c. lemon juice
1/2 c. maraschino cherries,
   drained and chopped
3 9-inch graham cracker crusts

Mix together whipped topping, condensed milk, pineapple, walnuts and lemon juice on low to medium speed with an electric mixer. Stir in cherries. Spoon into crusts; cover and chill. Makes 3 pies, 8 servings each.

It's easy to tote pies to a get-together...top off the filled pie plate with a lightweight vintage pie plate and secure the two with ribbon.

Desserts

Chocolate Fudge Pie

Julie Marsh
Shelbyville, TN

In memory of my mom Juanita Fears, I've created my own special traditions at Christmastime just as Mom did when I was little. This pie is one of them. The filling is so yummy, you can serve it without the crust!

5 T. baking cocoa
1 c. margarine, melted and
    cooled slightly
4 eggs, lightly beaten

1/2 c. all-purpose flour
2 c. sugar
1 t. vanilla extract
2 8-inch pie crusts

In a large bowl, combine cocoa, margarine and eggs. Add flour and sugar; mix well. Stir in vanilla. Divide evenly into crusts. Bake at 375 degrees for 30 minutes. Makes 2 pies, 6 to 8 servings each.

As Christmas rolled around each year, my mother would have us children crack the English walnuts she used in various recipes...nut bread, fruitcake and a little sweet we called Stuffed Dates. We younger children were each given a hammer and some walnuts, and we cracked them on a newspaper spread out on the kitchen floor. The shells that we managed to keep intact were set aside, and later, when all the nuts were cracked, we hurried to float them on water in the bathroom sink. They became our little "boats" and we used our imaginations. Sometimes we took them with us into the bathtub at bath time too. So it was great fun to crack the nuts and float our little boats, all part of a memorable childhood at Christmastime. My sister, who is now a grandmother, uses the walnut halves in a different and charming way. She fills them with trinkets or treats and glues them together for her grandchildren's Christmas stockings.

-Teresa Amert, Upper Sandusky, OH

Eggnog Cake

Jeanette Busby
Dedham, MA

*A rich treat to enjoy by a crackling fire. Top individual servings
with a sprinkle of nutmeg or cinnamon if you like.*

18-1/4 oz. pkg. yellow cake mix
  with pudding
3 eggs, beaten

1/3 c. oil
1 t. nutmeg
1-1/3 c. eggnog

In a large bowl, blend together all ingredients until smooth. Pour into
a Bundt® pan that has been sprayed with non-stick vegetable spray.
Bake at 350 degrees for 45 to 55 minutes, until a cake tester comes
out clean. Cool on a wire rack 10 minutes. Transfer to a nice plate.
Drizzle Eggnog Glaze over cake. Makes 12 servings.

Eggnog Glaze:

2 c. powdered sugar
2 T. margarine, softened

1 t. vanilla extract
3 to 4 T. eggnog

In a medium bowl, combine all ingredients except eggnog. Add
enough eggnog to reach a glaze consistency.

Small drawstring bags sewn of holiday print fabric
are sweet table favors. Fill them with packets of
flavored tea or coffee for a special surprise.

Desserts

Lemon Fluff

Janice Reinhardt
Bethel Park, PA

*This dessert was especially enjoyed by my dad. I would bake it
for his birthday celebrations. Dad is no longer with us,
but this cake always brings back fond memories of him.*

18-1/4 oz. pkg. lemon cake mix
8-oz. pkg. cream cheese,
   softened
3-oz. pkg. cream cheese,
   softened

3 c. milk
2 3.4-oz. pkgs. instant lemon
   pudding mix
12-oz. container frozen whipped
   topping, thawed

Prepare cake mix according to package instructions; bake in a greased
and floured 13"x9" baking pan. Let cool. Beat cream cheese with an
electric mixer. Add milk and pudding mixes. Beat for 5 minutes, then
spread over cooled cake. Top with whipped topping. Cover and
refrigerate; serve chilled. Serves 12 to 15.

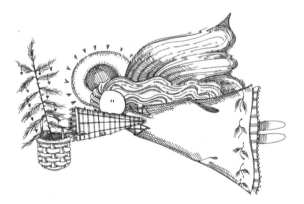

Christmas is not a time nor a season,
but a state of mind.
To cherish peace and goodwill,
to be plenteous in mercy,
is to have the real spirit of Christmas.

-Calvin Coolidge

Ice Cream & Cookie Dessert

Suzanne Ruminski
Johnson City, NY

Anything that I can make ahead for the Christmas holiday is so helpful! This frozen dessert is refreshing and goes well with all the Christmas cookies I serve. You can also substitute coffee-flavored liqueur for the crème de menthe...mmm, good!

18-oz. pkg. chocolate sandwich
   cookies, divided
1/2 c. margarine
3 1-oz. sqs. unsweetened
   baking chocolate
3 eggs, beaten

2 c. powdered sugar
1/4 c. crème de menthe
1/2 gal. vanilla ice cream,
   softened
2 to 3 drops green food coloring

Set 5 cookies aside for the topping. Crush remaining cookies and arrange in the bottom of a lightly greased 13"x9" baking pan. In a double boiler, combine margarine, chocolate, eggs and powdered sugar. Cook and stir until it thickens to a fudge-like consistency. Pour over cookies; cover and freeze for 20 minutes. In a bowl, fold crème de menthe into softened ice cream. Add food coloring for extra color. Spread over crust. Crush reserved cookies; sprinkle on top. Cover and freeze until serving time. Let stand a few minutes to soften before cutting. Serves 12.

Try using refrigerated chocolate chip or sugar cookie dough
to make a pie crust for a chilled filling or even for ice cream.
Pat dough into a pie plate, chill for thirty minutes,
then bake as package directs.

Desserts

Fastest Cheesecake

Erin Brock
Charleston, WV

This sinfully rich dessert is part of our New Year's Day tradition. No waiting overnight for good cheesecake. Just fifteen minutes to toss it together and an hour to chill. What could be easier? The secret is sweetened condensed milk...make sure you don't use evaporated or it won't turn out.

8-oz. pkg. cream cheese,
    softened
3-oz. pkg. cream cheese,
    softened
14-oz. can sweetened
    condensed milk, divided

1/4 c. lemon juice
9-inch chocolate cookie crust
Garnish: whipped cream,
    raspberry preserves

In a medium bowl, beat cream cheese with an electric mixer until smooth and fluffy. Gradually add half of condensed milk, beating constantly. When half of milk has been added, beat in lemon juice until smooth. Beat in remaining condensed milk until smooth. Pour into crust; cover and chill at least one hour. Garnish with whipped cream and raspberry preserves to serve. Makes 8 to 10 servings.

A simple lap quilt is a sweet way to preserve the memories in children's outgrown clothing. Cut large squares and stitch together, then layer with thin batting and a fabric backing.

Dark Chocolate Cake

Debbie Hubbard
London, KY

I had never made a cake from scratch before trying this delicious recipe. It is really simple and definitely worth the time...I'll be making it for my family again!

2 c. boiling water
1 c. baking cocoa
2-3/4 c. all-purpose flour
1/2 t. salt
2 t. baking soda

1/2 t. baking powder
1 c. butter, softened
2-1/4 c. sugar
4 eggs
1-1/2 t. vanilla extract

In a medium bowl, whisk together boiling water and cocoa until smooth; cool. In a separate bowl, sift together flour, salt, baking soda and baking powder. In a large bowl, blend together butter and sugar until light and fluffy. Beat in eggs, one at a time, mixing well after each addition. Add flour mixture, cocoa mixture and vanilla. Stir together and spread evenly in a well-greased 10"x8" baking pan. Bake at 350 degrees for 25 to 30 minutes. Makes 8 servings.

Who can resist marshmallow icing? Spoon a 7-ounce jar of marshmallow creme into a bowl and gradually beat in 3/4 cup softened butter. Beat in 3/4 teaspoon vanilla extract and 1/2 cup powdered sugar. Spread or pipe onto cookies for a billowy delight!

Desserts

Judy's Christmas Cake

*Judy Lange
Imperial, PA*

A yummy holiday favorite! So easy and so good!

18-1/2 oz. pkg. yellow cake mix
1/2 c. butter, melted and slightly
   cooled
3 eggs, divided
8-oz. pkg. cream cheese,
   softened

16-oz. pkg. powdered sugar
Garnish: additional powdered
   sugar

In a bowl, combine dry cake mix, butter and one egg; mix well. Add cream cheese, remaining eggs and powdered sugar; beat well. Pour into an ungreased 13"x9" baking pan. Bake at 350 degrees for 30 to 35 minutes. Let cool. To serve, sprinkle with additional powdered sugar. Serves 12.

Save those leftover shirt boxes for the next church bake sale or school party. Cut X's into the box tops and insert cupcakes into the openings...so easy to carry!

No-Bake Fruitcake

Christy Bonner
Berry, AL

This recipe was handed down to me by my Great-Aunt Georgia.
I love it because it's not your usual fruitcake. It's a real treat!

16-oz. pkg. graham crackers,
  crushed
2 c. candied red cherries,
  quartered
2 c. candied green cherries,
  quartered

2 c. raisins
2 c. sweetened flaked coconut
2 c. chopped pecans
14-oz. can sweetened
  condensed milk
16-oz. pkg. marshmallows

In a large bowl, combine graham crackers, cherries, raisins, coconut
and pecans; set aside. In a medium saucepan over low heat,
combine sweetened condensed milk and marshmallows. Stir until
marshmallows are melted; pour over graham cracker mixture.
Combine thoroughly. Press mixture into 3 wax paper-lined 9"x5" loaf
pans. Cover and refrigerate until cool and firm. Remove from pans
and slice. Makes 3 loaves, 12 to 15 servings each.

Poinsettia cuttings make beautiful and festive accents.
To keep them fresh, dip the stems for one minute in
boiling water to seal in the sap. Tuck them in
napkin rings or arrange them in a bowl of
evergreen boughs on your tabletop.

Desserts

Quick & Easy Bread Pudding

Eleanor Dionne
Beverly, MA

*I have used this recipe for many years. It is quick
to make and very tasty for an end-of-meal dessert.*

3.4-oz. pkg. cook & serve
   vanilla pudding mix
1/4 c. sugar, divided
3 c. milk, divided
1 T. butter

1/2 t. vanilla extract
6 slices dry bread, cubed
1/4 t. cinnamon
1/8 t. nutmeg

Combine dry pudding mix and 2 tablespoons sugar in a saucepan.
Blend in 2 cups milk. Cook and stir over medium heat until mixture
comes to a full boil. Remove from heat and stir in butter and vanilla.
In a bowl, pour remaining milk over bread to moisten; stir in pudding
mixture. Pour into a lightly greased one-quart casserole dish. Combine
remaining sugar with spices. Sprinkle over pudding. Broil until sugar
is lightly golden and bubbly, about 4 to 5 minutes. Serve warm or
chilled. Serves 6.

Make gifts extra special with personalized ribbon. Use alphabet
stamps, an ink pad made for fabrics and a thin, matte-finish
ribbon. Place the ribbon on a paper towel, which will
absorb any excess ink, and stamp on initials or names.

Grandma's Kolachy Cookies

Jennifer Savino
Jolliet, IL

My grandma would bake trays of cookies every Christmas to give to each family. She used an array of jams she preserved from her garden as the Kolachy filling. My favorite was her raspberry jam. These cookies take a bit more effort than other cookies, but the end result is worth it. I hope you enjoy these as much as I do!

1 t. active dry yeast
2 T. warm water
2-1/2 c. all-purpose flour
1 T. sugar
1/2 t. salt

1 c. butter, softened
2 T. whipping cream, scalded
   and cooled
4 egg yolks, beaten
18-oz. jar raspberry jam

Dissolve yeast in warm water, about 110 to 115 degrees. In a separate bowl, sift together flour, sugar and salt. Cut in butter until coarse crumbs form. Mix in yeast mixture, cream and egg yolks. Cover and chill for several hours. On a lightly floured surface, roll dough to about 1/2-inch thick. Cut with a 2-inch round cookie cutter. Cover and let rise until double in size. Place on lightly greased baking sheets. Make a depression in center of each cookie and fill with jam. Bake at 350 degrees for 15 minutes. Makes about 3 dozen.

Toasted oats can take the place of chopped nuts in cakes and cookies, adding crunch and nutty flavor. Simply cook uncooked oats in a little butter until golden. Cool before adding to a recipe.

Desserts

Delicious Cut-Out Cookies

Kimberly Freeman
Mountain Grove, MO

My mom, sister and I would make these cookies every Christmas for friends and neighbors and of course, a few for ourselves. The kitchen was covered with flour, icing and sprinkles. We played Christmas music while decorating each one. After our work was completed, we would gather in the living room and watch A Christmas Carol *while we enjoyed eating our fresh-baked cookies.*

3 c. all-purpose flour
1 t. baking powder
1/2 t. cinnamon
1/4 t. nutmeg
1 c. butter, softened

1-1/4 c. sugar
1 egg, beaten
1 t. vanilla extract
Garnish: icing, candy sprinkles

Stir together flour, baking powder, cinnamon and nutmeg. In a separate bowl, blend butter with sugar until light and fluffy. Beat in egg and vanilla. Beat in flour mixture until well combined. Cover dough and chill 3 hours. Divide dough in half; roll out on a well-floured surface. Cut with cookie cutters. Place 2 inches apart on greased baking sheets. Bake at 375 degrees for 8 to 10 minutes, until lightly golden. Cool and decorate as desired. Makes 2 to 3 dozen.

For the prettiest cookies, shake sprinkles or
sanding sugar over wet icing. Let the icing dry for
ten minutes before shaking off the excess.

Jenn's Pistachio-Cranberry Cookies

Debbie Button
Jarrettsville, MD

Last year my daughter Jenn and I were experimenting with some of our cookie recipes. She came up with this combination since the nuts, cranberries and chocolate chips were being used in other recipes. Voilà! Perfect for including in a cookie basket as an alternative to the traditional chocolate chip cookie.

18-1/2 oz. pkg. yellow cake mix
2 eggs, beaten
1/2 c. oil
1/2 c. pistachio nuts, chopped

1/2 c. sweetened dried
cranberries
1/2 c. white chocolate chips

In a large bowl, combine dry cake mix, eggs and oil; mix well. Fold in nuts, cranberries and white chocolate chips. Drop by teaspoonfuls onto ungreased baking sheets. Bake at 350 degrees for 12 minutes, or until edges are lightly golden. Transfer cookies to a wire rack to cool. Makes about 3 dozen.

Découpage Mom's favorite cookie or candy recipe onto the lid of a tin, then line with a lacy napkin...a thoughtful container for delivering goodies to a lucky friend or relative.

Desserts

Annie's Crescent Cookies

Annie Johnson
Concord, OH

I've been making this recipe for about five years. Four times a year I go on various bus trips to nearby states with my girlfriends. I made these cookies once and now they ask for them every time we meet!

1 c. butter, softened
1/2 c. powdered sugar
1 t. vanilla extract
1-3/4 c. all-purpose flour

1 c. chopped pecans
Garnish: additional powdered
  sugar

In a bowl, blend butter and sugar with an electric mixer on medium speed until smooth. Beat in vanilla. Gradually add flour with mixer on low speed. Fold in pecans with a spatula. Form dough into crescent shapes by tablespoonfuls. Place onto parchment-paper lined baking sheets. Bake at 275 degrees for 40 minutes. Cool slightly, then roll in additional powdered sugar. Remove to wire racks to cool completely. Makes 4 dozen.

Add sparkle to a holiday cookie tray...simply stir
some edible glitter into powdered sugar before
rolling balls of drop cookie dough.

Chocolate-Toffee Candy Cookies

Jennie Gist
Gooseberry Patch

*My mother-in-law Shirley used to make these
yummy, crunchy cookies every Christmas.*

36 saltine crackers
1 c. butter
1 c. brown sugar, packed

11-1/2 oz. pkg. milk chocolate
chips
1 c. chopped walnuts

Line a 15"x10" jelly-roll pan with aluminum foil; spray foil with non-stick vegetable spray. Arrange crackers in a single layer in pan; set aside. Combine butter and brown sugar in a medium saucepan over medium-high heat. Bring to a boil and boil for 3 minutes. Pour mixture evenly over saltines. Bake at 375 degrees for 5 minutes. Immediately sprinkle chocolate chips over top. Let stand for a few minutes; spread chocolate evenly with a spatula and sprinkle with nuts. Chill; break into pieces. Makes 3 dozen.

No-bake sandwich cookies the children will love to make and eat! Mix one tablespoon finely chopped maraschino cherries into 1/3 cup marshmallow creme. Spread about one teaspoon between two vanilla wafer cookies.

Desserts

Man Bars

Sally Green
Westlake Village, CA

This is a secret recipe I tried to acquire for years. Last Christmas I finally received it from a friend. Now I would like to share it with everyone. They're easy to make and look great in a Christmas tin. Enjoy them with coffee to really bring out their flavor.

2 c. graham cracker crumbs
6-oz. pkg. semi-sweet chocolate
   chips
1/2 c. walnuts, finely chopped

14-oz. can sweetened
   condensed milk
1 t. vanilla extract
Garnish: sugar

Mix together all ingredients except garnish. Pour into a well-greased 8"x8" baking pan. Bake at 350 degrees for 30 to 35 minutes. Cut into small squares and roll in sugar before serving. Makes about 1-1/2 dozen.

Starting when my oldest son was about three years old, every Christmas Eve we sprinkle reindeer oats on the ground and leave cookies and milk for Santa. Around ten that evening, I wake my two boys up to tell them that I have heard a noise. We look outside and there he is, Santa! Santa comes in, eats some cookies and starts unloading some presents, saying each of our names. Then, EVERY year, his ears perk up and he thinks he's heard something! We run back to bed, all excited! Santa has even walked around the neighborhood lightly ringing his bells. Luckily, all parents have been told via email to keep an eye out for him at a certain time. It's been a huge hit every year. Sadly, my husband is never around when all of this action is going on. But he loves hearing how excited the kids were to see the big man himself!

-Jennifer Bloch, Mount Airy, MD

Honey-Kissed Chocolate Cookies

Lisa Engwell
Bellevue, NE

My youngest daughter loves these cookies and begs to make them every year. Both my girls help roll the cookie dough in the sprinkles and then top them with a chocolate drop. And with no eggs in the batter, they can lick the bowl too!

1 c. honey
6 T. butter, softened
2 c. all-purpose flour
1 c. baking cocoa

1/2 t. baking soda
red and green sprinkles
3 doz. milk chocolate drops,
  unwrapped

In a medium bowl, beat honey and butter until light and fluffy. Beat in flour, cocoa and baking soda. Place sprinkles in a separate bowl. With hands, shape dough into one-inch balls. Drop balls into sprinkles and roll gently to coat. Place balls on baking sheets that have been sprayed with non-stick vegetable spray. Gently press one chocolate drop into the center of each cookie. Bake at 350 degrees for 10 minutes. Remove to wire racks to cool. Makes 3 dozen.

Make cookie giving fun...tuck lots of wrapped cookies inside a big Christmas stocking!

Desserts

Emily's Gingerbread Cookies

Vickie

This came from an elementary class assignment of my daughter Emily. She unscrambled words to uncover the recipe...she wrote "flower" instead of "flour." I still have the paper and treasure it!

1/3 c. brown sugar, packed
1/3 c. shortening
2/3 c. molasses
1 egg, beaten
3 c. all-purpose flour
1 T. baking powder

1-1/2 t. ground ginger
1/2 t. salt
Garnish: raisins, icing, licorice, red and green candy-coated chocolates, sprinkles

Blend together brown sugar and shortening until light and fluffy. Beat in molasses. Add egg, beating well. In a separate bowl, sift together flour, baking powder, ginger and salt. Add flour mixture to sugar mixture; mix well. Cover and refrigerate for 2 hours. Divide dough into fourths. Roll out to 1/4-inch thickness. Cut with cookie cutters. Place on greased baking sheets. Bake at 350 degrees for 5 to 7 minutes, until dark golden. Cool slightly on pans before removing to wire racks to cool completely. Decorate as desired. Makes 2 dozen.

In baking, 3/4 cup of sugar plus 1/4 cup of water can be substituted for one cup of molasses. Be sure to increase the spices to make up for the loss of the rich molasses flavor.

Powdered Sugar Sandies

Holly Child
Parker, CO

My mom makes these cookies around Christmas every year. My first year away to college in a cooking dorm, I baked these cookies and delivered them to my friends around campus before heading home for the holidays.

1 c. margarine, softened
1-1/2 c. powdered sugar,
   divided
1 t. vanilla extract

2-1/4 c. all-purpose flour
1/4 t. salt
Optional: 3/4 c. chopped
   walnuts

Mix together margarine, 1/2 cup powdered sugar and vanilla. Add flour, salt and nuts, if desired. Mix well. Form dough into one-inch balls and place on ungreased baking sheets. Bake at 400 degrees for 10 to 12 minutes. Place remaining powdered sugar in a bowl. Roll warm cookies in powdered sugar; let cool and roll again. Store in an airtight container once completely cooled. Makes 2 to 3 dozen.

Cookie exchanges are even more fun when guests bring copies of their recipes for sharing. As a special holiday surprise, make a cookie cookbook, and mail a copy to each guest. What a nice way to remember all of the festivities during a blustery January!

Desserts

Grandmother's Christmas Cookies
Stacey Peterson
Huntingburg, IN

This is my great-grandmother's recipe. For as long as I can remember, these were made only at Christmas to share with family & friends. My brother and I looked forward to them every year. Now, I make them with my kids!

1 c. butter, softened	1-1/2 t. baking soda
2 c. sugar	2 T. milk
3 eggs, beaten	5 c. all-purpose flour
1 t. anise extract	1-1/2 t. cream of tartar

Beat butter thoroughly. Add sugar a little at a time and blend thoroughly. Add eggs and extract. Dissolve baking soda in milk; add to butter mixture. Sift flour with cream of tartar. Add flour mixture to butter mixture; mix well. Turn out onto a floured board. Roll to 1/2-inch thick. Cut into desired shapes. Place on lightly greased baking sheets. Bake at 450 degrees for 7 minutes. Makes 4 dozen.

A sweet gift mix...Chocolate Chunk Hot Cocoa!
Combine these ingredients in an airtight container...2 cups baking cocoa, 3/4 cup sugar, 8 ounces chopped semi-sweet baking chocolate. Directions: In a saucepan, whisk 1/4 cup cocoa mix with 3/4 cup milk. Bring to a simmer. Makes one serving.

Eggnog Fudge

Gina McClenning
Nicholson, GA

Wonderful nibbling for Christmastime!

2 c. sugar
1 c. eggnog
2 T. butter
2 T. light corn syrup
1/4 c. chopped pecans, toasted

1/4 c. slivered almonds, toasted
 and chopped
1/2 c. candied red cherries,
 chopped
1 t. vanilla extract

Combine sugar, eggnog, butter and corn syrup in a heavy 4-quart saucepan. Cook over medium heat, stirring constantly, until mixture comes to a boil. Wash down crystals from sides of pan using a pastry brush dipped in hot water. Insert a candy thermometer into mixture. Cook, stirring occasionally, until mixture reaches the soft-ball stage, or until a candy thermometer reads 238 degrees. Remove from heat and cool, undisturbed, until temperature reaches 190 degrees, about 15 to 18 minutes. Stir in nuts, cherries and vanilla. Beat with a wooden spoon until fudge thickens and just begins to lose its gloss, about 5 to 8 minutes. Line a 8"x4" loaf pan with aluminum foil; coat with butter. Pour mixture into pan. Cool completely; remove from pan and cut into squares. Makes one dozen.

Thrice as nice…choose three coordinating ribbons
of different widths, stack them and tie all at once
around a special package.

Desserts

Traveling Fudge

Paula Bonchak
Bonham, TX

I have been sending goodies to Iraq for a couple of years so no matter how far away, our military can have a taste of home. One of the big hits, especially at Christmas, is this fudge. It arrives fine and everyone loves it. I thought I'd share Traveling Fudge so others can send some too.

3 c. sugar
1 c. evaporated milk
1/2 c. butter
12-oz. pkg. semi-sweet
   chocolate chips

1 c. marshmallow creme
1 t. vanilla extract
Optional: 1 c. coarsely chopped
   pecans or walnuts

In a heavy 5-quart Dutch oven over medium heat, bring sugar, milk and butter to a rolling boil, stirring until sugar dissolves and mixture begins to boil. Cook, stirring constantly to prevent scorching, to the soft-ball stage, or 234 to 243 degrees on a candy thermometer. Remove from heat. Stir in chocolate chips and marshmallow creme until melted and well blended. Add vanilla and nuts, if desired. Pour into a buttered 13"x9" baking pan. Cool and cut into squares. Store in an airtight container. Makes 2-1/2 to 3 pounds.

Fudge cut-outs are oh-so-simple to make and really dress up a dessert tray. Pour hot fudge into a jelly-roll pan and chill. Use mini cookie cutters to cut out stars, trees and other holiday shapes, then press on candy sprinkles. So sweet!

Peppermint Bark

Andrea Gordon
Lewis Center, OH

I started out making this recipe for family & friends for Christmas, but it turned out so good I make it year 'round!

2 12-oz. pkgs. white chocolate
   chips

1 t. peppermint extract
1/2 c. candy canes, crushed

In a microwave-safe bowl, heat chocolate chips in microwave for 30 seconds; stir, then heat for another 30 seconds. Stir extract and crushed candy into melted chocolate. Pour onto a parchment paper-lined baking sheet. Refrigerate for 2 hours; break into pieces. Store in an airtight container. Makes 10 to 12 servings.

Candy Cane White Hot Chocolate

Debbie Manning
Wayland, IA

A perfect comfort drink for when you're taste-testing a tray of Christmas cookies!

12 c. milk
9 1-oz. sqs. white baking
   chocolate, chopped
1 c. peppermint candy, crushed

1/4 t. salt
Garnish: whipped cream,
   additional crushed
   peppermint candy

Bring milk to a simmer in a large, heavy saucepan over medium heat. Reduce heat to medium-low. Add white chocolate, candy and salt; whisk until smooth. Ladle hot chocolate into mugs. Top with whipped cream and additional candy. Serves 12.

Licorice Caramels

Angie Whitmore
Farmington, UT

Growing up, Dad would buy us Callard & Bowser licorice toffee. I got this recipe from my sister and it's as close as I can get to that original toffee taste. It's always a part of our Christmas celebration.

2 c. sugar
1-1/2 c. light corn syrup
1 c. butter
14-oz. can sweetened
    condensed milk

2-1/2 t. licorice or anise extract
1/2 t. black food coloring

In a large heavy saucepan, combine sugar, corn syrup, butter and condensed milk. Stirring constantly, cook over medium heat to soft-ball stage, or 234 to 243 degrees on a candy thermometer. Remove from heat; stir in extract and food coloring. Line a 13"x9" baking pan with parchment paper; coat with butter. Pour mixture into pan. Cool at least 4 hours to overnight. Remove from pan and cut into 1/2-inch squares; wrap pieces in waxed paper or paper candy wraps. Makes 2-1/2 pounds.

Set aside leftover candy canes for Valentine's Day decorations!
Unwrap and arrange on parchment paper-lined baking sheets.
Form pairs into hearts by placing them hook to hook and tail to
tail. Bake at 350 degrees for 2 to 4 minutes, until they stick
together when the ends are lightly pinched. Let cool, tie with
ribbon and hang from windowpanes...so cheery!

Molasses Popcorn Balls

*Cindy Beach
Franklin, NY*

I remember going to my grandma's farm in the Catskill Mountains of upstate New York for Christmas. She would hang these popcorn balls from her Christmas tree in small plastic bags tied with curling ribbon. She would also have brown paper bags in every kitchen corner just full of them! Now I live in the same Catskill Mountains and carry on her tradition.

12 c. popped popcorn
1 T. butter, softened
1/2 t. salt

1 c. molasses
1/2 c. sugar

Place hot popcorn in a large bowl. Mix in butter and salt. In a small heavy saucepan over medium-low heat, bring molasses and sugar to a full boil. Boil until mixture reaches the hard-crack stage, or 290 to 310 degrees on a candy thermometer. Gradually pour mixture over popped corn; mix well. Shape into balls with well-buttered hands and cool on wax paper. Makes 9 to 10 balls.

Need a gift for a special family? Give a board game or a couple of card games along with a tin filled with homemade popcorn balls...it'll be much appreciated on the next snow day!

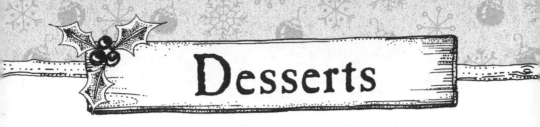

Desserts

Grandma's Peanut Brittle

Janet Haynes
Bowling Green, KY

Everyone looked forward to receiving my grandmother's peanut brittle as part of their Christmas gift. People still ask me for her recipe, even after thirty years!

3 c. sugar
1 c. light corn syrup
1/2 c. water
1-1/2 c. raw peanuts

1/2 c. butter, softened
3 T. baking soda
1/2 t. salt

Mix sugar, corn syrup and water in a heavy saucepan over medium heat. Continue to cook, stirring constantly, until mixture reaches the hard-ball stage, or 250 to 269 degrees on a candy thermometer. Add peanuts and cook until it reaches the hard-crack stage, or 290 to 310 degrees. Remove from heat. Stir in butter, baking soda and salt. Pour into an ungreased 15"x10" jelly-roll pan. Cool and break into pieces. Makes 2 dozen servings.

Add some jingle cheer! Slip a plastic zipping bag of Grandma's Peanut Brittle inside a red paper sack, fold the top over and punch holes across the top in one-inch intervals. Thread a large needle with thin ribbon and weave through the holes to close, adding jingle bells along the way.

Chocolatey Coconut Bars

Sheila Murray
Tehachapi, CA

*So good & easy! A must for us at Christmas. Santa will love
to find these at your kitchen table!*

2 c. graham cracker crumbs
1/2 c. sugar
1/2 c. butter, melted
2 c. sweetened flaked coconut

14-oz. can sweetened
  condensed milk
12-oz. pkg. semi-sweet
  chocolate chips

Mix together graham cracker crumbs, sugar and butter; press into the
bottom of an ungreased 13"x9" baking pan. Bake at 350 degrees for
7 to 8 minutes. Mix coconut and condensed milk. Spread on top of
baked crust. Bake at 350 degrees for an additional 15 minutes.
Meanwhile, melt chocolate chips in a saucepan over low heat. Spread
over top of bars. Cool; cut into bars. Makes about one dozen.

Make teddy bears for the
grandchildren from Grandpa's
soft flannel shirts. Whether you
use the simplest pattern or
a more elaborate one, they'll
treasure these endearing
reminders of Grandpa.

Royal Coconut Creme

Dorothy McConnell
Brooklyn, IA

It just isn't Christmastime with my husband's family
without this very rich and creamy candy.

3 c. sugar
6 T. butter, softened
1-1/2 c. whipping cream

1/8 t. salt
1 t. vanilla extract
2 c. sweetened flaked coconut

In a heavy saucepan over medium-high heat, bring sugar, butter, cream and salt to a boil. Stir mixture until it reaches the soft-ball stage, or 234 to 243 degrees on a candy thermometer. Remove from heat and let stand for 5 minutes. Stir in vanilla. Beat until thick and creamy. Mix in coconut. Pour into a buttered 13"x9" baking pan. Cover and let stand overnight. Cut into bite-size pieces to serve. Makes 2 pounds.

A recipe for success...always make candy just one batch at a time. Don't be tempted to double or triple the recipe, because the candy may fail to set up properly.

Texas Tumbleweeds

Marcia Smith
Round Rock, TX

No one can ever get enough of these candies. I bet you can't eat just one! This recipe can be easily halved, but you'll wish you had made more!

2 11-oz. pkgs. butterscotch chips
1/2 c. creamy peanut butter

4 c. shoestring potatoes
2 c. broken pecan pieces

Place butterscotch and peanut butter in a microwave-safe bowl. Microwave on high for one-minute intervals, until melted and smooth. Add the shoestring potatoes and mix until well-coated. Stir in pecans. Drop by teaspoonfuls onto aluminum foil-lined baking sheets. Refrigerate until candies harden. Remove from foil and store in a covered container in the refrigerator until serving time. Makes about 3 to 4 dozen.

For many years in California I held an annual Christmas tea. Almost three years ago I moved to Tennessee. The tradition has lived on here in my new home with new friends coming to tea. One year, about one and a half hours before tea, there was a knock at the door. When I opened it I was so stunned...I didn't even recognize my best friend of almost fifty years! She had surprised me by catching a red-eye flight and flying across country to be at tea. What a pleasant surprise to slow down for a few days during the holiday season and spend time with my best friend. It was the BEST Christmas present and will be talked about for years!

-Carolyn Tate, Clarksville, TN

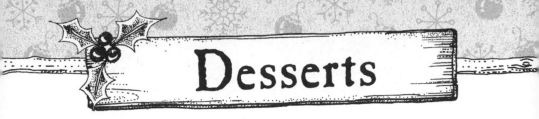

Desserts

Truffle Trios

Kristan Vaughn
Gooseberry Patch

*I teach Sunday school at church and these cookie truffles were
given to me in a gift basket at Christmastime. What a terrific treat!*

16-oz. pkg. chocolate sandwich
   cookies
8-oz. pkg. cream cheese,
   softened

2 8-oz. pkgs. semi-sweet
   baking chocolate, melted
1 c. powdered sugar
2 c. nuts, finely chopped

Remove cookie cream centers to a bowl; set aside. Crush cookie
wafers in a separate bowl; set aside. Add cream cheese to cream
centers; blend well. Add cookie crumbs to cream center mixture; mix
until blended. Roll cookie mixture into 42 balls, each about one-inch
in diameter. Dip 14 balls into melted chocolate. Roll 14 balls into
powdered sugar. Roll remaining balls in nuts. Place on parchment
paper-lined baking sheets and refrigerate until firm, about one hour.
Store truffles, covered, in refrigerator. Makes 3-1/2 dozen.

A chocolate truffle tree..how irresistible! Simply use
toothpicks to attach truffles or fudge candies to a
foam cone until the cone is completely covered.

Peppermint Ice Cream

Tori Willis
Champaign, IL

Christmas to me: sitting in front of the Christmas tree after decorating it, my mum sitting in my dad's lap, Christmas carols on the radio, us kids lined up on the couch each with a bowl of peppermint ice cream, no one saying a word, just admiring the glow of the pretty lights and the twinkle of tinsel...magical!

1 c. milk	1/2 t. vanilla extract
2/3 c. sugar	1/2 t. peppermint extract
2 c. whipping cream	2/3 c. candy canes, crushed

Whisk together milk and sugar until sugar is completely dissolved. Add cream and extracts. Pour into an ice cream maker. Churn about 20 to 25 minutes according to manufacturer's instructions, until thick and creamy. Add candy canes; churn an additional 5 minutes. Makes 1-1/2 quarts.

Grandma Ruth's Hot Fudge Sauce

Abby Kramer
Asheville, NC

Ever since I was a little girl, at Christmastime my mom would make this hot fudge sauce and buy peppermint ice cream to go with it. It is absolutely to die for!

1-1/2 1-oz. sqs. unsweetened baking chocolate	1/4 c. sugar
1/2 c. water	1/8 t. salt
2/3 c. sweetened condensed milk	peppermint ice cream, pudding or cake

Stirring constantly with a whisk, heat chocolate and water in the top of a double boiler over medium heat. Cook and stir until chocolate is melted, about 3 minutes. Add condensed milk, sugar and salt. Cook until thick and smooth. Serve over peppermint ice cream, pudding or cake. Serves 6.

Overnight Sausage & Egg Casserole
Cheri Emery
Quincy, IL

This is a great recipe for Christmas morning. Turn on the slow cooker right before you go to bed and it's ready for you when you wake up!

14 slices bread, quartered
1 lb. ground pork breakfast
    sausage, browned and
    drained
2-1/2 c. shredded Cheddar
    cheese

1 doz. eggs, beaten
2-1/4 c. milk
1-1/2 t. salt
1 t. pepper

In a greased slow cooker, arrange several layers of bread, sausage and cheese, ending with a cheese layer. Beat together eggs, milk, salt and pepper. Pour egg mixture over all. Do not stir. Cover and cook on low setting for 8 to 10 hours. Serves 6 to 8.

Every Christmas afternoon my mom would wash two of her wedding china teacups. She and Dad would sit down together, have their coffee and watch us play. Now that my sister and I are grown and have husbands and children of our own, we also sit down together and have coffee in Mom's china.

-Kim Hartless, Forest, VA

Slow Cooker

Make-Ahead Scrambled Eggs

Kathy Grashoff
Fort Wayne, IN

*Try this for your next holiday brunch. The beauty is you can
put it in a slow cooker and keep it warm for four hours!*

8 slices bacon
8-oz. pkg. sliced mushrooms
3 T. butter
16 eggs
1 c. half-and-half or milk
1/2 t. salt
1/4 t. pepper

10-3/4 oz. can cream of
  mushroom soup
2 T. fresh chives, chopped
4 Italian plum tomatoes,
  quartered and sliced
2 c. shredded Cheddar cheese

In a skillet over medium heat, cook bacon until crisp. Reserving one
tablespoon drippings in skillet, drain bacon on paper towels; crumble
and set aside. Add mushrooms to drippings in skillet; cook 4 to
5 minutes, until tender, stirring frequently. Remove from skillet; set
aside. Wipe skillet clean with a paper towel. Melt butter in same skillet
over medium heat. Beat eggs in a large bowl. Mix in half-and-half or
milk, salt and pepper. Add egg mixture to skillet; cook over medium
heat until firm but still moist, stirring occasionally. Stir in soup and
chives. Place half of egg mixture in a 3-1/2 or 4-quart slow cooker.
Top with half each of cooked mushrooms, tomatoes, cheese and
crumbled bacon. Repeat layers. Cover and keep warm on low setting
for up to 4 hours. Makes 12 servings.

Favorite ornaments getting lost
on a big tree? Gather them to
decorate a petite tabletop tree
and set it where you
often pass by.

Hot Spinach Dip

Beth Kramer
Port Saint Lucie, FL

The perfect appetizer for a New Year's Eve party! Just toss the ingredients into a slow cooker and set aside to warm up, while you make the rest of your holiday spread. Yummy with warm sourdough bread, cut into cubes.

2 10-oz. pkgs. frozen chopped
   spinach, thawed and drained
16-oz. jar jalapeño-flavored
   pasteurized process cheese
   sauce

10-3/4 oz. can cream of
   mushroom soup
3-oz. pkg. cream cheese,
   softened
2 T. dried, minced onion

Combine all ingredients in a slow cooker that has been sprayed lightly with non-stick vegetable spray. Cover and cook on low setting for about 2 hours, until hot. Stir a few times during cooking time to blend well. Keep warm and serve from slow cooker. Makes 6 to 8 servings.

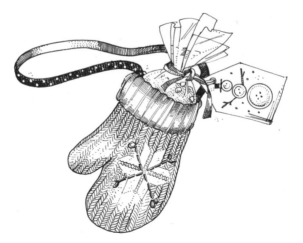

Send party guests home with whimsical goodie bags.
Fill store-bought mittens with wrapped candies, a bag of
roasted almonds and a note of thanks for coming!

Cheesy Sausage Dip

Emily Jordan
Sophia, NC

Last year for Christmas, my mom made me a cookbook with recipes from my great-great-grandmas, great-grandmas, grandmas, distant relatives, aunts and even my uncle. The book is a treasure and I love it dearly. This recipe was shared by my dad's cousin Lisa. It's a staple when my best friends and I get together for a sleepover or for movie night.

1 lb. ground pork sausage
16-oz. pkg. pasteurized process
   cheese spread, cubed

1-1/4 c. salsa
tortilla chips, sliced party
   rye bread

Brown sausage in a skillet over medium heat; drain. Place sausage in a slow cooker. Add cheese. Pour salsa over top. Cover and cook on low setting for 1-1/2 to 2 hours. Serve with tortilla chips or party rye bread. Serves 8 to 10.

Reuse empty plastic containers, potato chip cans and coffee tins into holiday gift containers. Just clean, dry thoroughly and wrap in pretty gift paper or decorate with last year's Christmas cards.

Vegetable Beef Soup

Diane Cohen
The Woodlands, TX

*Easy, good and makes the whole house
smell delicious as it's cooking!*

1 lb. ground beef, browned and
   drained
2 c. tomato juice

2 c. beef broth
16-oz. pkg. frozen mixed
   vegetables

Combine all ingredients in slow cooker. Cover and cook on high
setting for 3 hours. Reduce to low setting; cover and cook for an
additional 3 to 4 hours. Makes 4 to 5 servings.

This year, tuck sparkling beaded necklaces into
stockings...they're surprisingly easy to make! Beads can be
found at craft shops, and thin ribbon or silk beading cord
come in endless colors. Clasps are attached to the ribbon
at each end with a simple knot.

Slow Cooker

Simple Stew for Two

Kristin Gill
San Clemente, CA

If possible, stir this wonderful stew every two hours.
At the grocery store, you'll find the envelope of stew beef
seasoning mix with the gravy mixes.

14-oz. can beef broth
2 T. stew beef seasoning mix
1 lb. stew beef, cubed
16-oz. pkg. frozen mixed
    vegetables

Optional: 1 to 2 potatoes, peeled
    and diced

Mix together broth and seasoning in a slow cooker. Stir in beef, vegetables and potatoes if using. Add water if needed to cover vegetables. Cover and cook on low setting for 8 hours. Serves 2.

Fill pint-size Mason jars with red cinnamon candies and nestle a votive in the center. They'll look so welcoming lighting the walkway to your door.

Linda's Cheatin' Chili

Linda McWilliams
Fillmore, NY

My kids love chili, but who has time to make it? I created this recipe myself and it tastes like it's made from scratch. They'll think you spent hours preparing this homemade chili but it only takes about fifteen minutes!

2 lbs. ground beef
2 14-1/2 oz. cans diced
   tomatoes
1-3/4 oz. pkg. chili mix
1 c. spaghetti sauce
24-oz. jar chunky salsa
16-oz. can light red kidney
   beans, drained and rinsed

16-oz. can dark red kidney
   beans, drained and rinsed
1 to 2 c. water
Garnish: shredded Cheddar
   cheese, sour cream

In a skillet, brown ground beef; drain. To a slow cooker, add beef, tomatoes with juice and remaining ingredients except garnish. Cover and cook on low setting for 5 to 6 hours. Garnish as desired. Serves 8.

When you share a pot of homemade chili with neighbors, include a stack of bowls tied with a festive ribbon. A warming welcome on the first snowfall.

Buffalo Chicken Wing Soup

Anna McMaster
Portland, OR

*This spicy, creamy soup warms you up from your toes
to your nose on a cold winter day!*

6 c. milk
3 10-3/4 oz. cans cream of
　 chicken soup
3 c. chicken, cooked and
　 shredded

1 c. sour cream
1/4 to 1/2 c. hot pepper sauce
Garnish: shredded Monterey
　 Jack cheese, chopped green
　 onions

Combine all ingredients except garnish in a 5-quart slow cooker. Cover
and cook on low setting for 4 to 5 hours. To serve, garnish with
cheese and onions. Serves 8.

Crisp, savory crackers are delightful alongside a steamy bowl
of soup. Spread saltines with softened butter and sprinkle with
Italian seasoning and garlic powder. Bake at 350 degrees for
just a few minutes, until golden.

Broccoli & Cheese Casserole

Kristy Markners
Fort Mill, NC

A deliciously simple side dish to take to
family dinners...there's never any left!

10-oz. pkg. frozen chopped
   broccoli, cooked and drained
1/2 c. butter, melted
1-1/3 c. cooked rice

8-oz. jar pasteurized process
   cheese sauce
10-3/4 oz. can cream of
   mushroom soup

In a bowl, combine all ingredients. Spoon into a greased slow cooker.
Cover and cook on low setting for 4 hours. Makes 6 to 8 servings.

When slow-cooker side dishes like Broccoli & Cheese Casserole
are just about done, whip up a speedy chicken go-with. Simply
pound chicken breasts until thin, coat both sides in flour and
sprinkle on a bit of seasoning salt. Add a tablespoon of oil to a
skillet and cook for 3 minutes per side, until juices run clear.

Slow Cooker

Corn Pudding

Betty Kozlowski
Newnan, GA

I was glad to find this slow-cooker recipe to use during the holidays when the oven is in use full-time.

2 10-oz. cans corn
2 16 oz. cans creamed corn
2 8-1/2 oz. pkgs. corn muffin
  mix

1/2 c. margarine
8-oz. container sour cream

Combine undrained corn and remaining ingredients in a slow cooker. Cover and cook on low setting for 2 to 3 hours, until set. Makes 10 to 12 servings.

For the best deals on holiday decorations, shop in November! Outdoor decorations are marked down early in the month, indoor ones in the middle and tree trimmings after Thanksgiving.

Slow-Cooker Baked Eggplant

Megan Brooks
Antioch, TN

My sister brought this side to Christmas dinner a couple years ago. Who knew eggplant was the perfect accompaniment to ham? We now include it as part of our traditional meal. Capers give this dish a little extra zing. Sometimes I even toss in a few pitted olives for more flavor.

1 eggplant, peeled and cut into
   one-inch cubes
2 onions, thinly sliced
2 stalks celery, cut into
   one-inch pieces
1 T. olive oil
16-oz. can diced tomatoes
3 T. tomato sauce

1 T. sugar
2 T. balsamic vinegar
1 t. dried oregano
Optional: 1 T. capers, drained
salt and pepper to taste
Garnish: grated Parmesan
   cheese

Combine eggplant, onions, celery, oil, undrained tomatoes and tomato sauce in a slow cooker. Cover and cook on low setting 3 to 4 hours, until eggplant is tender. Stir in sugar, vinegar, oregano and capers, if using. Season with salt and pepper. Cover and cook on low setting 45 minutes to one hour, until heated through. Garnish with Parmesan cheese. Makes 4 to 6 servings.

Clean-up is a snap when you use disposable votives!
Place tealight candles in red or gold cupcake foils...simply toss
the foils when the wick is snuffed.

Turkey Dressing

Nancy Fenton
Stillwater, MN

There's nothing better than homemade dressing,
but this one is a very close second!

1 lb. ground turkey, browned
   and drained
1/2 c. butter
2 c. celery, chopped
2 c. onion, chopped

3 c. chicken broth
2 eggs, beaten
14-oz. pkg. sage &
   onion-flavored croutons

Place turkey in a slow cooker. Melt butter in a saucepan over medium heat; sauté celery and onion until tender but not browned. Add to slow cooker. Add remaining ingredients, mixing well. Cover and cook on high setting for 45 minutes. Reduce heat and cook on low setting for 4 to 5 hours. Stir every 45 minutes to avoid burning around the edges. Serves 10.

Spoon stuffing into hollowed-out peppers, tomatoes,
sweet onions or even acorn squash halves and bake.
It's an extra-special presentation on a buffet.

Cheesy Corn

Karen Kidd
Abilene, TX

*My family has never really liked vegetables, so I am always
looking for something they all will eat at holiday celebrations.
They love this and ask for "that corn stuff" each year.*

3 16-oz. pkgs. frozen corn
8-oz. pkg. cream cheese, cubed
1/2 c. butter, cubed
3 T. milk

3 T. water
2 T. sugar
6 slices American cheese,
　quartered

Mix together all ingredients in a slow cooker that has been lightly
sprayed with non-stick vegetable spray. Cover and cook on low
setting for 4 hours. Stir occasionally, adding a little more water if it
begins to stick. Serves 6 to 8.

Patty's Au Gratin Potatoes

Patty Hart
Eugene, MO

*I'm sharing this recipe in memory of my niece Lindsey. It was her very
favorite and she always asked me to bring it to family get-togethers.*

32-oz. pkg. frozen shredded
　hashbrowns
2 12-oz. containers sour cream
2 10-3/4 oz. cans cream of
　mushroom soup
1/4 c. milk

chopped onion to taste
seasoned salt and pepper
　to taste
6 to 9 slices American cheese
1/2 c. butter, sliced

Combine all ingredients except cheese and butter in a large bowl.
Mix well. In a slow cooker, alternate layers of the hashbrown mixture
and cheese, beginning and ending with the hashbrowns. Top with
butter. Cover and cook on high setting for 1-1/2 hours; turn to low,
cook 2-1/2 hours longer, or until potatoes are tender. Makes 8 to
10 servings.

Slow Cooker

Unfried Refried Beans

Kristy Markners
Fort Mill, SC

Mexican is my favorite food of all time! This is one of my new easy slow-cooker sides. It makes a bunch and the leftovers are just as good as the first bite! If you can't find chili salt, just substitute one teaspoon salt plus 1/2 teaspoon chili powder.

16-oz. pkg. dried pinto beans
1 t. chili salt

4-oz. can chopped green chiles

Soak beans in water overnight. Drain beans and place in a slow cooker. Add water to cover 2 inches over beans. Stir in remaining ingredients. Cover and cook on high setting for 8 hours. Drain off all but about 1/4 cup water. Use an immersion blender to blend until smooth. Serves 8.

Cut leftover wrapping paper scraps into small squares and découpage them to a shoebox, patchwork-quilt style. Tuck in holiday cards and family pictures you received this season. A keepsake you'll enjoy for years to come!

Slow-Cooker Potatoes

Marsha Konken
Sterling, CO

*For a hearty main dish, just add cubed cooked ham
to this creamy recipe...tasty!*

32-oz. pkg. frozen shredded
   hashbrowns, partially
   thawed
2 10-3/4 oz. cans Cheddar
   cheese soup

13-oz. can evaporated milk
1 c. green pepper, diced
2.8-oz. can French fried onions,
   divided

Spray a slow cooker with non-stick vegetable spray. Add hashbrowns, soup, milk, green pepper and all but 1/4 cup of onion rings. Stir to combine. Cover and cook low setting for 6 to 8 hours, or on high setting for 3 to 4 hours. Sprinkle with remaining onions just before serving. Serves 6 to 8.

A little washable poster paint and a brush is all that's needed to write cheery holiday greetings on mirrors or windows. And with a little soapy water, it will easily wash off after the holidays.

Slow Cooker

Festive Apples & Squash

JoAnna Nicoline-Haughey
Berwyn, PA

*I love the aroma of the spices throughout the house
while this is cooking!*

4 lbs. butternut squash
2/3 c. butter, melted
1 c. light brown sugar, packed
1/2 t. salt
3 T. all-purpose flour

1 t. cinnamon
1/2 t. ground ginger
1/2 t. nutmeg
6 Granny Smith apples, peeled,
  cored and sliced

Cut squash in half; remove seeds, peel and cut into 1/2-inch cubes.
Combine butter, brown sugar, salt, flour and spices; mix until crumbly.
Layer half of squash in an oval slow cooker. Top with half of the
apple slices and half of the spice mixture. Repeat layers. Cover and
cook on low setting for 6 hours, or on high setting for 3-1/2 hours.
Serves 6 to 8.

Keep all of your family's favorite holiday storybooks
in a basket by a cozy chair. Set aside one night as
family night to read your favorites together.

Barbecue Goose Sandwiches

Regina Vining
Warwick, RI

Each year we try to include goose at our Christmas dinner.
Our family keeps expanding, so I'm always looking for quick & easy
recipes. This one even lets us stick to our family tradition!

1/4 c. butter
2 cloves garlic, minced
1 yellow onion, sliced
2 goose breasts

3 to 4 c. chicken broth
3 T. Worcestershire sauce
16-oz. bottle barbecue sauce
4 to 6 buns, split

Melt butter in a large skillet over medium heat. Add garlic and onion
and sauté for 5 minutes. Add goose breasts and brown on both sides.
Place meat into a slow cooker that has been sprayed with non-stick
vegetable spray. Add broth to cover; stir in Worcestershire sauce.
Cover and cook on high setting for 6 to 8 hours, until meat shreds
easily. Remove to cutting board; remove bones and shred with
2 forks. In a bowl, combine meat with barbecue sauce. Serve on
buns. Makes 4 to 6 servings.

Antique thread spools can be made into old-fashioned
candleholders...tuck in a small taper, add holly berries,
sprigs of greenery and a bow.

Slow Cooker

Italian Sammies

Cynthia Malm
Clovis, CA

My family loves this dish and asks for it on almost every occasion they can think of. Since it's made in the slow cooker, I can spend time with the family instead of working in the kitchen all day and missing the fun! At one gathering, my brother had three servings and then took the leftovers home. His wife reported that he was very stingy and ate most of it up before she could even get to it!

3 to 4-lb. beef round or rump
   roast
1 T. paprika
16-oz. jar pepperoncini

1 yellow onion, chopped
1 T. garlic, minced
8 to 12 French rolls, split
Garnish: favorite condiments

Rub roast with paprika. In a slow cooker, add roast, pepperoncini with juice, onion and garlic. Cover and cook on low setting for 6 to 8 hours. Shred roast. Serve warm on split rolls. Garnish as desired. Serves 8.

Realistic snow for your Christmas village!
Simply lay lengths of rolled cotton along the ground
and rooftops, then sprinkle with crystal snow.

Tangy Ham Steaks

Stephanie Mayer
Portsmouth, VA

*The ham is juicy, tender and full of flavor...and the green beans
make it a whole meal. The simplest holiday dinner ever!*

1/4 c. brown sugar, packed
1 t. garlic powder
1 t. salt
1/4 t. pepper

2/3 c. cider vinegar
4 t. Worcestershire sauce
2 lbs. ham steaks
2 c. green beans

Combine all ingredients except ham and beans in a large bowl. Add
ham; stir to coat. Cover and refrigerate one hour to marinate. Add
ham and brown sugar mixture to a lightly greased slow cooker. Place
green beans over ham. Cover and cook on low setting for 8 to
10 hours or on high setting for 4 to 6 hours. Serves 4 to 6.

Tie different lengths of ribbon to Christmas-shaped
cookie cutters and hang them from a curtain rod...just
the right touch for the kitchen window.

Cola Ham for a Crowd

Lauren Williams
Kewanee, MO

Always a favorite at any of our family gatherings...especially Christmas. The ham falls off the bone, has wonderful texture and is so delicious.

12-oz. can cola   8-lb. bone-in ham

Place ham cut-side down in a large slow cooker, trimming to fit if needed. Pour cola over ham. Cover and cook on low setting for 8 to 10 hours. Makes 12 to 16 servings.

A special family tradition that we have held ever since our eldest was little is our Shepherds' Meal on Christmas Eve. We try to recreate what it may have been like for the shepherds that starry night so long ago. First, we make a big pot of lentil stew. The table is set with oil-burning lamps, sliced cheeses, sheepherder's bread and milk. Dad asks a special blessing over our simple meal. We thank God for sending His own dear Son, and allowing humble shepherds to be a part of the greatest event in history!

-Melisa Edge, Sequim, WA

Cranberry Turkey Breast

Patricia Wissler
Harrisburg, PA

This is so easy to make. The sauce is wonderful on mashed potatoes!

salt and pepper to taste
3 to 5-lb. turkey breast
16-oz. can whole-berry
    cranberry sauce

1.35-oz. pkg. onion soup mix
2 T. cornstarch
2 T. cold water

Sprinkle salt and pepper on turkey breast; place in a slow cooker. In a microwave-safe dish, heat cranberry sauce for 40 seconds to soften. Add onion soup mix to cranberry sauce; blend well. Spread cranberry mixture over turkey. Cover and cook on low setting 4 to 5 hours, until a meat thermometer registers 180 degrees. Remove turkey from the slow cooker and allow to rest for 10 minutes. While turkey is resting, cover the slow cooker and turn to high. In a small bowl, mix together cornstarch and cold water until smooth. When sauce is boiling, stir in cornstarch paste. Continue to simmer until it thickens. Slice turkey and serve with sauce. Serves 6 to 8.

Add a cozy glow to a nonworking fireplace. Cluster sets of twinkle lights inside, plug them in and enjoy the sparkling display!

Slow Cooker

Slow-Cooker Chicken & Noodles

Tam Schuster
Lexington, OH

*My husband, grown children and grandchildren
love this classic dish!*

3 to 4 boneless, skinless
   chicken breasts
2 10-3/4 oz. cans cream of
   chicken soup
4 10-1/2 oz. cans chicken broth

1/2 c. butter, sliced
1/2 to 1 t. garlic salt
1/4 t. pepper
dried parsley to taste
24-oz. pkg. frozen egg noodles

Combine all ingredients except noodles in a slow cooker. Cover and
cook on low setting for 8 hours. Remove and shred chicken; return to
slow cooker. Add frozen noodles; stir. Continue cooking on low for
one more hour. Serves 6 to 8.

Winter Chicken Stew

A quick go-with for a slow-cooker meal...toss steamed
green beans, broccoli or zucchini with a little olive oil
and chopped fresh herbs.

Coconut Curry Chicken

Dawn Salisbury
Pleasant Grove, UT

I love this recipe because it is something I can toss in the slow cooker in less than five minutes. My husband loves it because it's reminiscent of his time in New Zealand.

6 frozen boneless, skinless
   chicken breasts
14-oz. can coconut milk

2 T. yellow curry
cooked rice

Place chicken in a slow cooker. Mix together coconut milk and curry; pour over chicken. Cover and cook on low setting for 4 hours, or on high setting for one to 2 hours, until chicken juices run clear. Serve over rice. Serves 6.

Use a sturdy rubber band to secure peppermint sticks to the outside of a cylindrical vase. Tie on a pretty ribbon to cover the band and fill with a favorite holiday bouquet or candle...so easy!

Slow Cooker

Florence's Philippine Chicken

Jane Luke
Valrico, FL

My mother was shooed out of her mother's kitchen, so she learned to cook after she was married. She collected recipes from her friends that were easy and foolproof. I found this one in her recipe box when I was looking for recipes to make for my new husband when we got married. I like it because it's inexpensive and I always have the simple ingredients on hand.

8 chicken thighs
3 T. cider vinegar
3 T. low-sodium soy sauce

1 clove garlic, minced
1/8 t. pepper

Place chicken in a slow cooker. Combine remaining ingredients and pour over chicken. Cover and cook on low setting for 6 hours. Serves 4.

Small cheer and great welcome
make a merry feast!

-William Shakespeare

Garlic Chicken Alfredo

Laurel Perry
Loganville, GA

Even picky eaters will love this creamy dish.
And you'll love how easy it is!

16-oz. jar garlic Alfredo sauce, divided
4 to 6 boneless, skinless chicken breasts
4-oz. can sliced mushrooms, drained

cooked spaghetti or fettuccine pasta
Garnish: grated Parmesan cheese

Pour half of sauce into a slow cooker. Place chicken on sauce; top with mushrooms and remaining sauce. Cover and cook on low setting for 6 to 8 hours. Serve over pasta; garnish with Parmesan cheese. Serves 4 to 6.

An elegant centerpiece in a jiff! Place white candles in various sizes in a large bowl. Tuck in silver ornaments and strings of beads that spill over the edges.

Slow Cooker

Slow-Cooker Chicken Cacciatore

Denise Thom
Lake George, NY

An easy recipe to prepare for busy weeknights. It's nice to come home to a fragrant, hot dinner. I serve this chicken with a tossed salad and fresh garlic bread. A no-fuss meal that's so good!

1 onion, thinly sliced and
　separated into rings
2 boneless, skinless chicken
　breasts, diced
1 T. garlic, chopped
1 t. Italian seasoning
1 t. pepper

1/2 t. salt
28-oz. can crushed tomatoes
6-oz. can tomato paste
3/4 c. water
16-oz. pkg. angel hair pasta,
　cooked

In a slow cooker, layer onion, chicken, garlic, seasonings, tomatoes, tomato paste and water. Cover and cook on low setting for 6 to 8 hours. Serve over cooked pasta. Makes 6 servings.

Slip a prewarmed ceramic tile into the bread basket before adding a napkin liner. Biscuits and rolls will stay toasty and warm through dinner.

Mediterranean Pork Tenderloin

Andrea Treadwell
Orrington, ME

A four-ingredient dish that packs a lot of flavor!
Serve with a tossed vegetable & pasta salad.

1-1/2 to 2-lb. pork tenderloin
14-1/2 oz. can diced tomatoes
   with garlic and onions
2-1/4 oz. can sliced black olives,
   drained

8-oz. container crumbled feta
   cheese

Place pork in a slow cooker. Cover with tomatoes and olives. Sprinkle feta cheese on top. Cover and cook on low setting for 6 to 8 hours. Serves 6.

Give gift cards or movie passes tucked inside easy-to-make pouches. Fold a length of three-inch wide ribbon in half; stitch the long sides together. Trim the short edges with pinking shears and slip the gift inside.

Hoolipsey

Betty Jo Riendel
Stockton, CA

Hoolipsey, or "pigs in a blanket," was a tradition at Thanksgiving and Christmas. I have my Great-Grandmother Katrine's meat grinder, patented in 1875, that my mama used to grind the salt pork in the original recipe from the old country. When I was a little girl, I loved the Hoolipsey best the next day and just a little warm. Make sure to use ground pork, not sausage, for this recipe.

1 to 2 heads cabbage
1 lb. ground pork
1 white onion, chopped
1-1/2 c. long-cooking rice,
   uncooked

salt and pepper to taste
32-oz. jar sauerkraut, drained
   and juice reserved

Fill a large stockpot half full of water; bring to a boil over medium-high heat. Meanwhile, run a sharp knife around cabbage stems. Reduce water to simmering. Place cabbage stem-side down in stockpot; cover. Meanwhile, combine ground pork, onion, rice, salt and pepper in a large bowl. Pour reserved juice from sauerkraut over pork mixture. Drain cabbage; cool slightly. Remove wilted cabbage leaves and set aside. Put half of sauerkraut into a slow cooker. Wrap a tablespoon of pork mixture in each cabbage leaf; place in slow cooker. Cover with remaining sauerkraut. Cover and cook on low setting for 6 hours. To serve, gently uncover pork rolls from under sauerkraut and remove to a serving platter. Serve with sauerkraut. Serves 10.

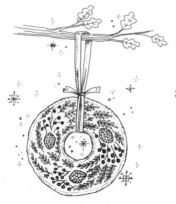

For a magical ice wreath, arrange cranberries and pine trimmings in a ring mold and fill with water. Freeze until solid, then pop out of the mold. Hang outdoors from a tree branch with a sturdy ribbon.

Wacky Beef Roast

Lauren Anderson
Grand Rapids, MI

The gravy from this zesty roast is wonderful on mashed potatoes.
Use any leftovers for hot roast beef sandwiches.

2 to 3-lb. beef chuck roast
1-oz. pkg. ranch dressing mix
.7-oz. pkg. Italian dressing mix

.87-oz. pkg. brown gravy mix
1/2 to 1 c. warm water

Place roast in a slow cooker. Combine dry dressing and gravy mixes; sprinkle on top of roast. Pour in warm water. Cover and cook on low setting for 6 to 8 hours. Serves 6.

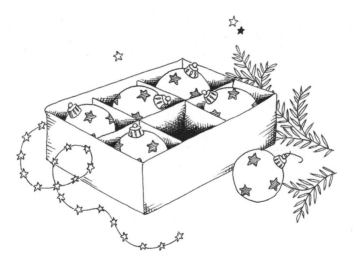

When it's time to take down the tree, set aside the unbreakable round red ornaments for your summer garden! Hang them on tomato plants early in the season. When birds come to peck, instead of yummy tomatoes, they'll find the hard bulbs and leave your plants alone by the time the real fruits ripen.

Slow-Cooker Roast with Mushrooms

Gloria Kaufmann
Orrville, OH

It's great coming home on a fall or winter evening to smell a roast in the slow cooker. Cook the noodles and a vegetable while setting the table and you've got a meal that's good enough for company.

2 to 3-lb. beef chuck roast, trimmed and cut into thin strips
12-oz. pkg. sliced mushrooms
1 onion, chopped
1-1/2 t. salt
1/2 t. pepper
2 T. cornstarch
2 T. cold water
1/2 c. sour cream
1 T. Dijon mustard
cooked egg noodles

Combine beef, mushrooms, onion, salt and pepper in a slow cooker. Cover and cook on low setting for 8 hours, or until beef is tender. Turn off slow cooker. Whisk together cornstarch and water. Remove one cup of liquid from slow cooker and combine with cornstarch mixture. Return to slow cooker; cook until thickened. Stir in sour cream and mustard. Serve over noodles. Serves 5.

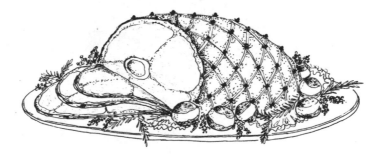

Cooking for a crowd? Roasting meats can easily be doubled in a large slow cooker. Add only half again as much seasoning, not twice as much...otherwise flavors may be too strong.

Halibut with Tomatoes

Jen Thomas
Santa Rosa, CA

I've been trying to sneak more fish into my family's diet and this recipe is so good even the kids like it. This version is perfect for a winter meal...even for Christmas with all the red and green. But you can also fix it with fresh tomatoes and basil in the summer.

4 6-oz. halibut fillets
14-oz. can peeled Italian plum
    tomatoes, drained and
    chopped
1 T. tomato purée

1 green pepper, chopped
garlic salt to taste
cracked pepper to taste
1 t. dried basil

Arrange fish fillets in a slow cooker that has been sprayed with non-stick vegetable spray. In a bowl, stir together remaining ingredients; pour over fish. Cover and cook on low setting for 3 to 5 hours. Serves 4.

Gourd snowmen look sweet on a tabletop...they're an easy party craft too. Simply paint bottle gourds with white craft paint and let dry, then paint on features. Add a strip of fleece for a neck scarf and pull on a tiny baby sock for a cap.

Citrus Party Fish

Mia Rossi
Charlotte, NC

My family's version of the traditional Italian fish dinner!
We like to serve this quick & easy (and might I add tasty!) dish
on Christmas Eve, just before opening presents.

1-1/2 lbs. tilapia fillets
salt and pepper to taste
5 T. fresh parsley, chopped
1 onion, chopped
4 t. oil

2 t. lemon zest
2 t. orange zest
Garnish: orange and lemon
  slices

Season fish fillets with salt and pepper; place in a lightly greased slow cooker. Place parsley, onion, oil and zest over fish. Cover and cook on low setting for 1-1/2 hours. Garnish with orange and lemon slices. Serves 6 to 8.

A crisp green salad goes well with all kinds of slow-cooked main dishes. For a zippy lemon dressing, shake up 1/2 cup olive oil, 1/3 cup fresh lemon juice and a tablespoon of Dijon mustard in a small jar and chill to blend.

Baked Apples with Caramel

Beth Holcomb
Webb City, MO

My grandmother made these tasty apples on cold days in the fall.
They became a special treat whenever she had extra apples
and it was raining outside.

4 tart apples, cored
1/2 c. apple juice
1/2 c. brown sugar, packed
12 red cinnamon candies
1/4 c. butter, softened

8 caramels, unwrapped
1/4 t. cinnamon
Garnish: whipped cream or
vanilla ice cream

Peel the top of each apple; place apples in a slow cooker side by side.
Pour juice over apples. Fill the center of each apple with 2 tablespoons
brown sugar, 3 cinnamon candies, one tablespoon butter and
2 caramels. Sprinkle with cinnamon. Cover and cook on low setting
for 4 to 6 hours, until apples are tender. Serve immediately, garnished
as desired. Makes 4 servings.

When the holidays are over, save those extra candy canes.
Use as stirrers to infuse coffee and tea with peppermint,
or crush them to add a minty layer to s'mores.

Slow Cooker

Apple Peanut Crumble

Charlotte Smith
Tyrone, PA

*An absolutely wonderful dessert! Turn on the slow cooker
while getting the rest of your meal ready for guests.*

4 to 5 baking apples, peeled,
   cored and sliced
2/3 c. brown sugar, packed
1/2 c. quick-cooking oats,
   uncooked
1/2 c. all-purpose flour

1/2 t. cinnamon
1/2 t. nutmeg
1/3 c. butter, softened
2 T. creamy peanut butter
Garnish: vanilla ice cream

Place apple slices in a slow cooker. Combine brown sugar, oats, flour,
cinnamon and nutmeg. Cut in butter and peanut butter. Sprinkle over
apples. Cover and cook on low setting for 5 to 6 hours. Serve warm
with vanilla ice cream. Serves 4 to 5.

Every year since I was born, my grandmother gave me a
Christmas ornament. Some were handmade, some were
store-bought, but each was picked out with a special meaning.
Her intention was that when I moved out and had my own tree,
I would have quite a nice collection. Now I buy myself special
ornaments. And when I pull out the boxes of decorations,
I remember each one that came from her. While trimming our
Christmas tree, my son loves hearing about every ornament
from his great-grandmother!

-Wendy Garwood, Northfield, NJ

Creamy Rice Pudding

Darlene Brown
Herndon, PA

I found this easy recipe in a farm newspaper some time ago. It's as creamy as rice pudding made in the oven or on the stovetop. To cook raisins, simply boil them in water for five minutes, drain and let cool.

9 c. whole milk
1 c. long-cooking rice, uncooked
1/8 t. salt
1 c. plus 1 t. sugar, divided

3 eggs, beaten
1 T. vanilla extract
Optional: 1 c. cooked raisins
Garnish: cinnamon

Combine milk, rice and salt in a slow cooker. Cover and cook on high setting for 2-1/2 to 3 hours. Stir every hour. After rice is cooked, stir and add one cup sugar. In a bowl, beat together eggs, remaining sugar and vanilla. Add to slow cooker. Cover and cook an additional 5 to 10 minutes, until heated through. Fold in raisins, if desired. Sprinkle cinnamon on top. Makes 6 to 8 servings.

Create a sweet candy land on your sideboard. Hot-glue
hard candy mints to foam cones from the craft store
and arrange around the dessert trays...how pretty!

Index

Index

Index

Have a taste for more?

We created our official Circle of Friends so we could fill everyone in on the latest scoop at once.
Visit us online to join in the fun and discover free recipes, exclusive giveaways and much more!

www.gooseberrypatch.com

Join Our Circle of Friends

Find Gooseberry Patch in Your Neighborhood

Find us on Facebook

You Tube

Follow us on twitter

Read Our Blog

Call us toll-free at 1·800·854·6673

U.S. to Canadian recipe equivalents

Volume Measurements

1/4 teaspoon	1 mL
1/2 teaspoon	2 mL
1 teaspoon	5 mL
1 tablespoon = 3 teaspoons	15 mL
2 tablespoons = 1 fluid ounce	30 mL
1/4 cup	60 mL
1/3 cup	75 mL
1/2 cup = 4 fluid ounces	125 mL
1 cup = 8 fluid ounces	250 mL
2 cups = 1 pint =16 fluid ounces	500 mL
4 cups = 1 quart	1 L

Weights

1 ounce	30 g
4 ounces	120 g
8 ounces	225 g
16 ounces = 1 pound	450 g

Oven Temperatures

300° F	150° C
325° F	160° C
350° F	180° C
375° F	190° C
400° F	200° C
450° F	230° C

Baking Pan Sizes

Square

8x8x2 inches	2 L = 20x20x5 cm
9x9x2 inches	2.5 L = 23x23x5 cm

Rectangular

13x9x2 inches	3.5 L = 33x23x5 cm

Loaf

9x5x3 inches	2 L = 23x13x7 cm

Round

8x1-1/2 inches	1.2 L = 20x4 cm
9x1-1/2 inches	1.5 L = 23x4 cm